DEAR DIRT DOCTOR

Dear Dirt Doctor

QUESTIONS ANSWERED
THE NATURAL WAY

HOWARD GARRETT

University of Texas Press ◆ Austin

Revised and updated edition of *The Dirt Doctor's Guide to Organic Gardening* (1995)
First revised edition, 2003

Requests for permission to reproduce material from this work should be sent to Permissions, University of Texas Press, Box 7819, Austin, TX 78713-7819.

⊗ The paper used in this book meets the minimum requirements of ANSI/NISO Z39.48-1992 (R1997) (Permanence of Paper).

Library of Congress Cataloging-in-Publication Data
Garrett, Howard, 1947–
  Dear dirt doctor : questions answered the natural way / Howard Garrett.
     p.   cm
Includes bibliographical references (p.   ) and index.
  ISBN 0-292-72847-6 (pbk. : alk. paper)
  1. Organic gardening.   2. Organic gardening—Texas.
3. Organic gardening—Miscellanea.   I. Title.
SB453.5 .G358   2003
635'.0484'09764—dc21
                                                    2003001912

Contents

Trees   105

DEAR DIRT DOCTOR

Introduction:
Basics of Going Organic

TEN REASONS TO GO ORGANIC

There are many reasons to go organic and stop using synthetic toxic pesticides and high-nitrogen artificial salt fertilizers, but here are the ten most important reasons.

1. *The organic program improves health.* Organic fertilizers, soil amendments, and pest control products improve the health of the microscopic life in the soil, the earthworms, the roots of plants, the top growth, and the overall production of plants. In addition, you, your family, and your pets don't have to be exposed to toxic chemical poisons. The organic method works within nature's laws and systems and is nontoxic to beneficial insects, birds, lizards, frogs, toads, earthworms, and other life. Pets and humans can be added to the list. Even the manufacturers of the toxic chemicals admit—in fact, brag about—the fact that their products kill all the bugs. That's right—they can't tell the difference between the good and the bad bugs.

2. *The organic program is cost effective.* Any project can be converted from toxics to organics at the same budget, but what is more important is that the costs are reduced every year in an organic program. Each year fewer sprayings for pests are needed, fewer dead plants have to be replaced, and plant production continues to increase. And what price do you put on your pets' health and your health? Beds never have to be removed and redone, as is often the case under chemical pro-

grams. Under an organic program, the soil gets better and better forever—just as the forest floor and the tall prairie grass do.

3. *Organic programs save time.* Because of the healthy soil, less irrigation is needed, less fertilizer is needed, and less frequent replacing of diseased and dead plants is needed. Doing these things less often saves time compared to the recommended synthetic schedule. Another time convenience is that the timing of the organic applications is not as critical. The season's first fertilization can go down whenever time allows after the first of the year; the second, whenever time allows in late spring to early summer, and the third, whenever time allows in the late summer through fall. Since the organic fertilizers aren't soluble, they can be broadcast basically anytime. The nutrients become available to the plant roots when the temperature and moisture conditions are right for the feeding of soil microbes. In the meantime, they stay in place and behave themselves.

4. *Organic programs result in sick and insect-infested plants less often.* When adapted plants are chosen and planted correctly in the proper place, they have few pests and require little care. High-nitrogen synthetic salt fertilizers and toxic pesticides are problem creators. They lead to more pest problems than anything else, partly because of the destruction of beneficial microbes and insects, but more importantly because of the weak, watery cells created by the fake fertilizers. Organic fertilizers and organic pest control techniques are problem solvers. They concentrate on stimulating health rather than on fast production.

5. *Organic programs provide greater summer heat tolerance.* Plants growing in soil that is rich in compost, rock minerals, and beneficial living organisms have a greater resistance to all stresses, including severe heat stress. Trace minerals are an important part of this stress tolerance. They are abundant and available to plants in an organic program. Organically grown plants have larger and more efficient root systems. The root systems respond even more than the top growth does, and they are the key to healthy plants.

6. *Organic programs provide greater cold tolerance.* When the

proper balance of organic matter, mineral nutrients, air, and living organisms is present in the soil, ornamental plants and food crops have a greater concentration of complex carbohydrates, or sugars, and these sugars create a natural antifreeze effect. Trace minerals again are a very important factor here. Many Texas organic growers have personally experienced these benefits. Freeze damage occurs on organically grown plants at a temperature significantly lower than on plants artificially grown.

7. *Organically grown fruits, vegetables, and herbs taste better.* The increased trace minerals and complex sugars in organically grown plants increase their taste. Taste is directly related to the health and nutrition of the food. So-called experts will argue this and other points of mine, but they are wrong. There's a very easy test. Eat fruits and vegetables grown both ways and see which you like better. Also, the use of toxic poisons eliminates, or should eliminate, the use of many foods and herbs. The best example is the rose. If you are not spraying poisons and dousing the surrounding soil with toxic synthetics, the petals are edible and are delicious in salads and teas, and the hips, which are the rose fruits, are delicious in teas and one of the best sources of natural vitamin C.

8. *Organic programs improve the environment.* Unlike synthetic fertilization, organic programs don't cause excess nitrogen to volatilize into the atmosphere nor soluble nutrients to leach through the soil and into the water stream. Organic fertilizers stimulate beneficial microorganisms, which very effectively clean up contaminations such as pesticides, excess mineral salts, and heavy metals in the soil. Leaching is reduced to almost nil, and no one has to breathe the fumes or otherwise come in contact with the toxic materials.

9. *Organic programs recycle valuable natural resources.* All once-living materials are rotted through composting and mulching and recycled back into the soil to build humus and trace minerals. Grass clippings are left on the turf, leaves are left as mulch in beds, tree trimmings are turned into mulch, and animal manures are composted to become important fertiliz-

ers. Under the synthetic programs, these valuable resources are often taken to landfills.

10. *Organics is more fun.* It's really no fun to spill toxic poisons all over yourself, breathe the fumes, or have to deal with the contaminated containers and residues. Under an organic program, the ease of application, the great diversity of life that's experienced, and the successful production of plants truly create some of life's great pleasures.

One of the most common questions I get relates to getting started. It usually goes something like this: "I've tried Texas A&M's chemical approach, and it isn't working. I'm ready to give the Natural Way a try. How do I start?" Here's how to make the conversion.

BASIC ORGANIC PROGRAM

STEP 1: Stop using all synthetic fertilizers and pesticides.
STEP 2: Start recycling organic matter, building soil health
    with organic products, composting, and mulching.
STEP 3: Use native plants and well-adapted introductions.

For those of you who are new to the Natural Way of thinking and for those of you who are veterans, here's an update on the Basic Organic Program, or the BOP for short. The more we learn, the simpler it gets.

Use Adapted Plants

Planting well-adapted plants is the most important step. Unless you select adapted plants, it doesn't matter whether your program is organic or toxic. The best choices are the natives, but the well-adapted introductions and naturalized plants are also good.

Encourage Biodiversity

Healthy gardens, farms, and ranches need a mix of plants and animals. Monocultures of plants are often very productive for a while, but later succumb to insects and diseases. Examples include the Irish potato blight, Dutch elm disease, and, more recently, oak wilt here in Texas. Monocultures lack the genetic diversity to respond to changing environmental threats and thus become sitting ducks for parasites, predators, and pathogens. Stop using all products that do damage to the life in the soil. Encourage life instead.

Build the Organic Matter

Use compost, earthworm castings, and organic fertilizers to build the organic matter or humus in the soil. Mulch all plantings. Maintain an organic mulch layer on the bare soil year-round. Avoid all synthetic fertilizers that contain no organic matter.

Build the Mineral Content

Balance the minerals in the soil by applying rock powders or sands that provide the major nutrients and trace minerals needed by plants to be healthy. Volcanic rock materials are especially important because they provide much more than minerals. The best choices include lava sand, Texas greensand, soft rock phosphate, granite sand, zeolite, basalt, and natural diatomaceous earth.

Planting

Prepare beds for ornamentals or food crops by scraping away existing grass and weeds. Toss the material into the compost pile. Spraying a herbicide first is an unnecessary, contaminating waste of money and time. Next add a 4–6-inch layer of compost, lava sand, or other volcanic material at 40–80 pounds per 1,000 square feet, organic fertilizer at 20 pounds per 1,000 square feet, wheat/corn/molasses amendment at 30 pounds per 1,000 square feet and till to a depth of 3 inches into the native soil. Excavation and additional ingredients such as concrete sand, peat moss, foreign soil, and pine bark should not be used. They are a waste of money and can hinder plant growth.

More compost is needed for shrubs and flowers than for

ground covers. Add Texas greensand at 40–80 pounds per 1,000 square feet to black and white soils and high-calcium lime at 50–100 pounds per 1,000 square feet to acid soils. Decomposed granite is an effective amendment for most soils. It can be used up to 100 pounds per 1,000 square feet.

Remove container-grown plants from their pots, rake the loose soil off the top of the ball, and set the plants in the new beds at a level slightly higher than the surrounding grade. Remove the cloth and excess soil from the top of balled and burlapped plants.

Mulching

Mulch all shrubs, trees, ground covers, and food crops with 2–5 inches of shredded native tree trimmings to protect the soil from sunlight, wind, and rain; inhibit weed germination; decrease watering needs; and mediate soil temperature. Other natural mulches can be used, but avoid Bermudagrass hay because of possible herbicide residue.

Fertilizing

Apply organic fertilizer 2–3 times per year. Foliar-feed during the growing season by spraying turf, tree, and shrub foliage; trunks; limbs; and soil at least monthly with Garrett Juice or other organic blends. Add volcanic sand such as lava sand, dry molasses, and humate to the soil the first few years.

Watering

Water only as necessary. The organic program will reduce the frequency and volume needed. Add a tablespoon of apple cider vinegar per gallon when watering pots. Do as often as time permits. Use 1 ounce of liquid humate per gallon of water in areas with acid soils and water.

Mowing

Frequency of mowing varies with grass varieties. Leave the clippings on the lawn to return nutrients and organic matter to the soil. Mulching mowers are the best but not essential. Put occasional excess clippings in compost pile. Do not ever let clippings leave the site. Do not use or allow maintenance people to use line trimmers around shrubs and trees. They can do serious damage to plants.

Weeding

Hand pull large weeds and work on soil health for overall control. Mulch all bare soil. Avoid synthetic herbicides, such as pre-emergents, broadleaf treatments, soil sterilants, and especially the SU (sulfonylurea) herbicides such as Manage and Oust, as well as Picloram and Clopyralid products. Spray broadleaf weeds as a last resort with full-strength vinegar with 2 ounces orange oil and 1 teaspoon of liquid soap or remove weeds by hand. Several commercial organic herbicides are now available, including Garden-Ville Organic Weed Control, Weed Eraser, Burn Out, and others. Some of these products contained diluted glacial acetic acid in the past. Use only products that contain natural vinegar or vinegar made from ethyl alcohol.

Pruning

Remove dead, diseased, and conflicting limbs. Do not over-prune or make flush cuts. Leave the branch collars intact, and do not paint cuts except on red oaks and live oaks in oak-wilt areas when spring pruning can't be avoided. Remember that pruning cuts hurt trees. For the most part, pruning is done for your benefit, not for the benefit of the trees.

Compost Making

Compost, nature's own living fertilizer, can be made at home or purchased ready to use. Compost can be started any time of the year in sun or shade, and its ingredients can include anything that was once living—grass clippings, tree trimmings, food scraps, bark, sawdust, rice hulls, weeds, nut hulls, animal manure, and the carcasses of animals. Mix the ingredients together and simply pile the material on the ground. See the "Compost" chapter for further information.

Compost Tea

Manure compost tea is an effective foliar spray because of its many mineral nutrients and naturally occurring microorganisms. Fill any container half full of compost and finish filling with water. Let the mix sit a few days and then dilute and spray on the foliage of any and all plants. Pumping air into the tea with a simple aquarium pump increases its power. How to dilute the dark compost tea before using depends on the compost used. A rule of thumb is to dilute the leachate down to one part compost liquid to 4–10 parts water. The ready-to-use spray should look like iced tea. Be sure to strain the solids out with old pantyhose, cheesecloth, or floating row-cover material. Full-strength tea makes an excellent fire ant mound drench when mixed with 2 ounces molasses and 2 ounces orange oil per gallon. Add vinegar, molasses, and seaweed to compost tea to make Garrett Juice.

Controlling Insects

Aphids, spider mites, whiteflies, and lacebugs: Release ladybugs and green lacewings regularly until natural populations exist. Spray Garrett Juice or garlic-pepper tea. Use strong water blasts for heavy infestations. **Caterpillars and bagworms:** Release trichogramma wasps. Spray Garrett Juice plus 2 ounces orange oil per gallon. Spray *Bacillus thuringiensis* (Bt) with 1 ounce molasses per gallon of spray as a last resort. **Fire ants:** Drench mounds with Garrett Juice plus orange oil, release beneficial nematodes, and go totally organic. **Grasshoppers:** Eliminate bare soil, apply beneficial nematodes, broadcast Nolo Bait for the young nymphs, and spray kaolin clay particle film if needed. Encourage biodiversity and feed the birds regularly. **Grubworms:** Beneficial nematodes and general soil health are the primary controls. **Mosquitoes:** Broadcast cedar flakes and use cedar mulch. Use *Bacillus thuringiensis* 'Israelensis' (Bti) for larvae in standing water that can't be drained. Spray orange-oil-based products or garlic-pepper tea for adult insects. Do not use toxic chemicals such as pyrethrins, pyrethroids, or DEET. Lavender, vanilla, citronella, and eucalyptus also repel mosquito adults. **Slugs, snails, fleas, ticks, chinch bugs, roaches, crickets:** Spray or dust natural diatomaceous earth products and broadcast cedar flakes and crushed red pepper. Orange-oil-based products also kill these pests. Research now shows that instant coffee at 1 ounce per gallon of spray is effective. For more details on pest control, check out the *Texas Bug Book*.

Controlling Diseases

For black spot, brown patch, powdery mildew, and other fungal problems, the best control is prevention through soil improvement, avoidance of high-nitrogen fertilizers, and proper watering. Spray Garrett Juice plus garlic, potassium bicarbonate, milk, or neem. Treat soil with horticultural cornmeal at about 20 pounds per 1,000 square feet. Organic gardens have few disease problems, but these natural techniques work well. Plants can also be sprayed with corn juice, which is made by soaking cornmeal in water (put the cornmeal in old nylon hose to keep the larger particles from the juice). The commonly recommended synthetic neurotoxins like Terrachlor, Daconil, Bayleton, and Funginex have no place in today's horticulture and agriculture.

Garlic-Pepper Tea Insect Repellent

In a blender with water, liquefy 2 bulbs of garlic and 2 cayenne or habanero peppers. Strain away the solids. Pour the garlic-pepper juice into a 1-gallon container. Fill the remaining volume with water to make 1 gallon of concentrate. Shake well before using and add ¼ cup of the concentrate to each gallon of water in the sprayer. To make garlic tea, simply omit the pepper and add another bulb of garlic. For additional power, add 1 ounce of seaweed and molasses to each gallon. Always use plastic containers with loose-fitting lids for storage.

Garrett Juice

For one of the best foliar sprays and soil drenches, mix the following per gallon of water: 1 cup of compost tea or liquid humate, 1 ounce liquid seaweed, 1 ounce blackstrap or any dark molasses, 1 ounce apple cider vinegar. To make a mild insect-control product, add 1 ounce citrus oil per gallon of spray. To make the fire ant killer, add 2 ounces citrus oil per gallon. When spraying the foliage of plants, don't use over 2 ounces citrus oil per gallon of spray. This mixture also works as a soil-detoxification product if you are just starting your organic program.

The above is a simplified version of the overall plan, but it should be helpful in giving you a good starting point. More details on each point are found further in the book.

Welcome aboard. I'm sure you will enjoy learning the Natural Way.

BALANCE OF CHEMISTRY, PHYSICS, AND BIOLOGY

Organic gardening is not just a matter of using different kinds of fertilizers and pesticides. Changing from Orthene, diazinon, Dursban, and Sevin to diatomaceous earth, garlic, hot pepper, and citrus oil is not the main objective. Neither is changing from Peters 20-20-20, Miracle-Gro, ammonium sulfate, and other high-nitrogen synthetics to cottonseed meal, manure compost, seaweed, molasses, and bat guano. More than just switching products, the organic method requires a complete change of attitude and a completely different thought process.

The synthetic chemical approach deals only with the chemistry of the soil. In so doing, it basically ignores the two other major pieces of the puzzle—physics and biology. Physics relates to the physical structure, texture, aeration, and drainage of the soil. Biology relates to the living organisms in the soil— the insects, microbes, and earthworms. Healthy soil must have a balance of chemistry, physics, and biology. Whatever is done to any of the three factors affects the other two. The chemical fertilizer approach doesn't even handle the chemistry properly because the synthetic fertilizers lack carbon and any useful amount of trace minerals. In addition, the physics and biology are completely ignored. If the chemistry is properly improved by using balanced fertilizer, the physics and biology will immediately improve. Improve the physics by aerating, and the biology and chemistry will improve. Improve the biology by adding biostimulants or actual living organism products, and the physics and chemistry start improving immediately.

The chemistry, physics, and biology of the soil are directly related, and it's extremely important that they be functioning properly. How do you use this knowledge effectively or apply this simple thought model? Ask yourself this question: If I use this product, fertilizer, soil amendment, or stimulant, will it benefit or hurt the earthworms? If only those products that benefit the living organisms are used, the soil fertility will improve with every application, and nature will balance the chemistry, physics, and biology for you.

The only testing lab in Texas that provides information on what nutrients are actually available to plants is Texas Plant and Soil Lab in Edinburg: 956-383-0739, www.txplant -soillab.com. Other labs use harsh acids to break down the soil into its basic elements. These tests offer no help on what nutrients are available. It is also the only testing lab to give organic fertilizing recommendations as a standard procedure.

Soil and Bed Preparation

Bed preparation is about improving the existing soil. No matter what the color, texture, or condition of the soil, it can be improved to a healthy condition. The basic process is the same regardless of whether the plot of land is a small urban garden or a large farm or ranch. We just have to be more careful with the costs on the larger properties. The only reason to bring in additional or new soil is if the grade is too low and must be raised. Otherwise, let's do the following:

1. Add compost.
2. Add volcanic rock sand.
3. Add cornmeal.
4. Add organic fertilizer.
5. Till or fork the amendments into the native soil.
6. Plant.
7. Mulch the bare soil with shredded mulch.

Only the amounts will vary. For ground-cover beds, about 2 inches of compost is needed, 4 inches for shrubs and vines, and up to 6 inches for perennials and hard-to-grow plants. Native perennials don't need any more than ground covers, but daylilies, roses, peonies, and other harder-to-grow plants need the heavier amounts of bed-preparation amendments.

Some plants will need special bed preparation if your soil is highly different from what they have in their native habitat. Dogwoods, camellias, and gardenias, for example, need heavy amounts of all the amendments, and azaleas need a totally different treatment. My favorite mix for these plants is 50 percent aged cedar flakes and 50 percent finished compost. Into each cubic yard of the mix add 5 gallons of lava or other volcanic sand and 1 gallon each of Texas greensand and horticultural cornmeal. Moisten the mix and pile it around the plants sitting on the top of the ground. For container-grown plants, be sure to sever the bound roots at the outside edge of the root balls.

BED PREPARATION

Q. How should we prepare the soil of a newly constructed home before the new St. Augustine turf is laid down?

A. All you need is a little compost ($\frac{1}{4}$–$\frac{1}{2}$ inches or so) or humate (10 pounds per 1,000 square feet) and rock powder like lava sand or decomposed granite (about 80 pounds per 1,000 square feet). Apply organic fertilizer to the top of the sod immediately after planting. Solid sod can be planted any time of the year it is available.

Q. I do not recall ever hearing you recommend adding earthworms to a garden or flower bed. Would they help the soil?

A. I highly recommend earthworms. They are the intestines of the soil. They aerate with their tunneling, they fertilize with their castings, they stimulate and increase the population of beneficial microorganisms in the soil, and they increase trace mineral availability to plant roots. You don't have to buy them, however—just use organic amendments such as compost, manure-based fertilizers, natural meals, lava sand, and Texas greensand, and they will appear. Build it and they will come. The most effective amendment of all for attracting earthworms is molasses—liquid or dry.

PLANTING IN SOLID ROCK

Q. If the site is basically all white rock, what's the best plan? Dig out the rock, bring in new soil? Add lots of compost or potting soil?

A. If solid, hard rock is on the surface, the only option is to bring in new soil. A clean, dark topsoil would be my favorite choice here. Take time to look at the material before you buy it. The term "topsoil" is grossly misused. Sold under this term are sand, dirt, contaminated soil, cushion sand, and other poor soil choices. As the term suggests, topsoil should come from near or on the surface of the ground. It should contain organic matter and trace minerals. Sandy loam would be the second best choice. It comes from deeper in the ground and has less organic matter and nutrient value. Sand is almost completely devoid of nutrients, dirt is contaminated soil of unknown origin, and cushion sand is the cheap orange-brown material that is used for new construction and building pads. Other than good-quality topsoil, none of these materials will grow plants well without amendments and added nutrients.

If the new site's soil is soft rock mixed with clay, it can be amended with the normal materials—compost, lava sand, Texas greensand, and organic fertilizers. The same goes for sites where a thin layer of soil covers the rock. That's exactly what our front yard in the Lakewood area of Dallas has.

In white limestone rock situations, the best plant choices are those natives that enjoy the high-calcium conditions—bur oak, Texas red oak, cedar elm, chinkapin oak, Texas ash, and native pecan. For small trees, pick from yaupon holly, rusty blackhaw viburnum, Carolina buckthorn, and Mexican buckeye. For the even smaller plants, native or introduced, improve the beds more by adding heavier amounts of the organic amendments, especially compost. Even with improved beds, the most successful landscaping results from the native perennials, ground covers, and vines. Well-adapted introductions such as crape myrtles, hollies, and nandinas are fine too, but the bulk of the plants should be natives.

MULCH

Mulch is organic material spread on beds and around plantings to protect the soil. Mulch helps to retain moisture and minimizes compaction caused by irrigation and rainfall. It blocks out sterilizing ultraviolet light and looks nice. Mulch helps to balance the temperature of the soil, keeping it cooler in the summer and warmer in the winter. And, as the mulch breaks down, it adds nutrients to the soil.

Nature doesn't allow bare soil and neither should you. Do

not use weed cloth. It interferes with the important soil/mulch interaction, and it doesn't work. It's just a waste of money.

Check with your city or local tree-care companies. Many make mulch available free or at a minimal cost.

Here are some common mulches in order of my preferences—and why.

Excellent

- Recycled material that grew on your own property: The best mulch of all.
- Shredded native tree trimmings: Excellent efficient choice.
- Shredded cedar: It's native, repels pests, and is the best choice to purchase.
- Shredded hardwood bark: A good choice for sloped areas and is the neatest looking of the shredded mulches.

Good

- Large-sized pine bark: It breathes and stays in place well. Some people don't like the look.
- Cypress chips: Expensive and can seal off oxygen. Also has to be shipped across the country. It's okay to use in Louisiana or Florida where it is produced.
- Pecan or peanut shells, rice hulls: Inexpensive but don't stay in place well. Fresh pecan shells will attract fire ants.

Poor

- Small- to medium-sized pine bark: Washes or blows away. When it stays in place, it can seal off oxygen. Produces strong growth-inhibiting natural chemicals—turpines, phenols, etc.

Terrible

- Peat moss: Expensive and blows or washes away. Slow to decompose to add nutrients to the soil.
- Plastic: Cooks the soil and plant roots and ruins the natural systems in the soil.

Mulch from Walnut

Q. I believe I understood you to say not to use walnut wood shavings, as they could kill plants. I want to check that information, as I have two bags of walnut shavings I was just about to use for mulch. If these shavings are not good to use as mulch, is there any way I can use them or should I just get rid of them?

A. Don't use them directly in the beds, but it is okay to mix them in the compost pile with other materials. Mix them with leaves and spent plants, add some dry molasses to the pile, and a wonderful topdressing mulch will be ready to use in a few weeks. Fresh walnut shavings by themselves will have a growth-retarding effect.

Q. I added about 4 inches of tree trimmings to my flower beds between Christmas and New Year's. I had put down corn gluten meal in late fall. Now I see from your calendar we'll need to put fertilizer, cornmeal, lava sand, and dried molasses on them this spring. Will I need to take all the mulch off to put that down?

A. No, just toss the material on top of the mulch, scratch it in lightly with a cultivating tool, and then water it into the mulch. In future, you can time the application of amendments to when the mulch has broken down and become thin. The amendments can then be added before the additional mulch is put down.

Rose-Bed Mulch

Q. I have recently read that you suggest alfalfa hay as mulch for roses. I have not been successful in locating this product. I was wondering if you could send me a list of suppliers in this area or close proximity that carry alfalfa hay.

A. Most of the feed stores and some of the organic garden centers carry alfalfa hay, but we now know that native cedar mulch is much better. It looks good, smells good, lasts longer, repels insects, helps with diseases, and encourages plant growth better than any other mulch. It also costs considerably less.

Mulch and Termites

Q. I just put in flower beds next to my house and would like to know which mulches besides stones don't attract termites.

A. The best mulch—and no, there is no problem with attracting termites—is shredded native cedar. Termites are on every property. They're supposed to be. Their job is to break down organic matter. We just don't want that organic matter to be your house.

Newspaper Mulch

Q. I have been using old newspapers for several years in my flower beds. As a weed preventative, it works great to put down a layer of paper and then add my top layer of hardwood mulch. Now I'm concerned because someone on HGTV said not to use newspaper with color print. Well, that's impossible. Every page has some color on it. Do they mean the slick ad inserts or everything? Should I stop using it? Have I destroyed my organic yard I've worked so hard for?

A. Those people don't know what they are talking about. Most of the color ink is soy based. It's the black ink that is petroleum based and sometimes contains some heavy metals. It's okay to use the newspaper, but I would compost it first and use it on ornamental plants instead of the food crops. Adding plenty of molasses to the compost pile will increase the heat from the microbe activity and better neutralize any contaminants.

Pecan Mulch

Q. We just bought a house with several large, beautiful pecan trees and are starting to lay out a new garden bed with compost tilled into the existing soil. Our neighbor told us to make sure that we don't include any pecan leaves in our compost, as they excrete a substance that acts as a natural herbicide. Is there any truth to the matter? And if so, how diligent do we need to be about keeping fallen leaves out of the compost and garden?

A. There is no problem at all using pecan leaves in the compost pile, but I would always mix several different raw materials together for best results. Walnut leaves and other walnut residue are a concern when used heavily around your garden plants, especially the nightshades like tomatoes, peppers, potatoes, eggplant, and tobacco. But pecan is no problem.

Q. My husband and I discovered a free source for pecan shells. We eagerly dumped them into our compost pile and, after some research in which we determined they were safe to use as mulch, put them in all the flower beds. This spring, my zinnia beds failed to reseed with the gusto they usually impart. Could the pecan shells have had some inhibitory effect on the germination of the zinnias, and on the growth rate of the annuals? I know walnut shells can be bad news, and it just occurred to me that perhaps the pecan shells were the culprit. The ones in the compost pile have broken down nicely, but those in the beds are still identifiable.

A. Raw pecan shells do seem to have a growth-retarding effect when mixed into the soil fresh, but I've always seen them to be effective in the soil after composting. They are good to use anytime as a topdressing mulch. This would be a good time for you to add the native cedar mulch and see the growth-improving qualities. A mix of wheat bran, cornmeal, and dry molasses would do a good job of getting all your bedding plants growing again. Use it at 20 pounds per 1,000 square feet. It's a good mild organic fertilizer for all plants.

Pine Needles

Q. Is it okay to use raw, uncomposted pine needles as a top-dressing mulch around trees, flowers, etc.?

A. Sure! Pine needles have gotten a bum rap from people who don't know what they are talking about. My parents, who live in Pittsburg, Texas, in the Piney Woods, use pine needles exclusively and have had great gardening success. The only negative about them is that they look a little out of place if you have no pine trees.

PEAT MOSS

Q. You don't recommend peat moss when preparing planting beds, yet you do recommend it for your potting soil. Please explain.

A. Good question. For some reason, probably the fluffiness of the material, peat moss does seem to help plants in containers. Without the peat moss, pots don't drain as well, and thus the plants don't have as much growth, flowering, and fruit. On the other hand, beds in the ground do not show increased production from the peat and do as well or better with only compost, rock powders, sugars, and organic fertilizers. Peat moss is very expensive, lifeless, nutrient lacking, and is an environmental problem because of the shipping needed to get the material to most of the country. Compost, on the other hand, is alive, loaded with nutrients, and inexpensive, and it recycles valuable local and regional natural resources, which keeps those materials out of the landfills. The fact remains, however, that some peat moss in the potting soil does seem to be beneficial.

But peat has a more important use. It is an excellent packing material for shipping fish and other food products and preventing their spoilage. The reason peat moss works so well for this use is that it is antimicrobial. That's why we don't use it instead of compost in beds. It does not encourage decomposition and life in the soil.

Q. In your planting quick tips, you advise not to use peat moss in bed preparation. My soil tests at 7.4, and I am trying to lower the pH organically. I would have thought peat would help, though I realize it is a nonrenewable resource.

A. If you really think that adjusting the pH is important, Texas greensand and vinegar are much better tools for lowering pH.

TREATED WOOD IN THE GARDEN OR LANDSCAPE

Q. We want to make frames for raised vegetable garden beds. I read on the Internet that one could stain wood with 50:50 linseed oil/mineral spirits to preserve the wood, even pine. Have you heard of this? We are debating whether to use wood or cinder blocks. Wood is easier but would not last as long. What do you recommend?

A. There's nothing good about using wood to retain soil. If there are enough toxic chemicals in the wood to prevent it from rotting, you don't want to touch it, much less eat food growing next to it. If there are not enough chemicals in the wood, it will rot.

Either way, it's a bad investment. I don't think the linseed oil and mineral spirits will last long either, especially in organic beds rich in decomposing microbes. You'll be surprised how well the raised beds will stay in place, even if the edges slope steeply. Use cider blocks or natural stone for permanent, low-maintenance walls. Lava sand put in the cinder block holes will keep the walls in place better, add paramagnetism (low-level natural energy), and hold moisture. Poured concrete can also be used. One more method is simply to mound the bed and slope the edges down at 45°. Beds built with lots of compost and mulched with shredded material will stay in place well.

P.S. Treated wood (CCA—copper chromated arsenate) has been taken off the market now, but the question remains—what to do about the existing structures? Ready Seal from Ready Products is a stain that locks the toxic heavy metals into the wood to prevent leaching and rubbing off onto clothes or skin. When removing the wood, it should be handled as toxic waste.

Q. I have a garden area where I kept old landscape timbers for several years. I would like to use this area as an herb garden. What should I do to neutralize any contaminants that might be present?

A. Buy and use the activated-carbon product NORIT, then drench the area with Garrett Juice and orange oil at 2 ounces per gallon. Living organism products such as Bio-Inoculant will also help. Mixing zeolite into the soil at 50 or more pounds per 1,000 square feet will also help with the decontamination process.

Q. What are your thoughts on using creosote railroad ties for a border around a vegetable garden?

A. They are highly toxic and should not be used. Use concrete or natural stone or simply mound the beds. When rich with compost and other organic amendments and covered with shredded mulch, mounded beds stay in place and produce well.

Compost

BASICS

Compost is nature's own living fertilizer that should be made at home but can be purchased ready to use. Simply put, it is decomposed once-living material.

A compost pile can be started any time of the year in sun or shade. The best container is no container—just a pile at some inconspicuous place on your property. If you must contain it, hay bales or concrete blocks are good choices. Wood is bad, as it rots.

Everything that was once alive should be composted. That includes all your garden waste and everything you bring to your property that was once alive. Most people readily accept that leaves, clean hay, grass clippings, tree trimmings, sawdust, rice hulls, weeds, nut hulls, and other vegetative materials can be composted. But some people get confused about two essential additions—food waste and pet waste.

All food waste—including meat scraps, other proteins, egg shells, and vegetable oils—should go in your pile. If it should-n't be composted, you shouldn't have been eating it. Pet waste belongs in your compost pile, not in a plastic bag at the curb headed for the landfill. If pet waste is dangerous to be around, it would be during the "fresh out of the animal stage," not after it has been composted.

Everything that was once alive should be composted. The ideal mixture of raw materials is about 80 percent brown stuff, like dry leaves, sawdust, and bark, and 20 percent nitrogen material, like animal manure, fresh vegetable waste, and green plant foliage. But any mix will compost.

Oxygen is a critical component, so it's best that the ingredients be a mix of coarse- and fine-textured material to promote air circulation through the pile. Turn the pile once a month if possible. Turning more often speeds up the process but also releases nitrogen into the air. If you don't turn it at all, it will compost eventually—in about a year.

Another critical component is water. A compost pile should be roughly the moisture of a squeezed-out sponge to help the living microorganisms thrive and work their magic.

Compost is ready to use when the ingredients are no longer identifiable. The color will be dark brown, the texture will be soft and crumbly, and it will have the fresh smell of the forest floor. Rough, unfinished compost can be used as topdressing mulch around all plantings. Use compost in all bed preparation.

Organic matter is the most important and possibly the most misunderstood tool of the organic program. Organic matter serves as a reservoir of nutrients and water in the soil, reduces soil compaction and surface crusting, and increases water infiltration into the soil. Organic material is anything that was alive and is now in or on the soil. Organic matter is the broken-down material we call humus. Humus is organic material that has been converted by microorganisms to a resistant state of decomposition. Organic material is unstable in the soil, changing form and mass readily as it decomposes. As much as 90 percent of it disappears quickly because of decomposition. Organic matter, on the other hand, is stable in the soil. It has been decomposed until it is resistant to further decomposition.

Organic material becomes humus through the natural process called composting.

COMPOST QUESTIONS

My three most common questions are: (1) What can and cannot go in the compost pile? (2) Where should the pile be located? and (3) What kind of container should be used?

The location answer is—anywhere, sun or shade. It can be indoors, outdoors, on the soil, or on concrete. On the ingredients question—anything that was once alive can and should go into the compost pile. The best way to neutralize old seed, weeds, diseased plants, dead insects, manure of any kind, kitchen scraps of any kind, and corpses of any kind is to compost them. Weeds and weed seed are loaded with minerals, often those that are lacking in the soil. If you want to make sure the pile heats up well and does a thorough job of neutralizing weed seed and other ingredients, add cornmeal or molasses to the pile. The amounts are not critical. People will say not to put greasy food from the kitchen in the pile. Well, let me tell you something—if it shouldn't go in the compost pile, you sure as heck shouldn't have been eating it!

Ants in Compost

To get rid of ants in the compost pile, all you have to do is add cornmeal and some molasses. The ants don't like either product, but the combination of them with the other ingredients in the pile, like dry leaves, food scraps, and moisture, will run the ants out quickly and help create a better compost. Both of these amendments superstimulate microbes in the pile. These beneficial microorganisms are the best of all fire ant controls. The ants know that fact and will hit the road.

Black Plastic Bag Composting

Q. Have you had any experiences with black plastic bag composting? My mother, due to back problems, has started this type of composting, using mainly grass clippings. The compost is very smelly and is not working out the way she thought it would. I compost with bins and am amazed at the results I get and love it. She is afraid if she goes that way it will be harmful for her back. Thanks.

A. The only problems are the small volume and the possibility of the bags catching on fire from the contained heat caused by the microbiological activity. Tell your mother that she doesn't have to turn the piles to get compost—it just takes longer.

More on Ingredients

Q. My husband and I are going round and round about what can and cannot go into a compost bed. He seems to think you can put meat scraps and such in, and I was taught that only garden clippings, grass, leaves, and vegetable waste should be used. Meat causes some sort of problem that I don't remember specifically what it is—probably flies and animals. I don't want a critter problem. I tried to find the info but couldn't find the meat issue addressed specifically.

A. Your husband is right—anything once alive can and should go in the compost pile. The only risk of attracting wild animals is if meat and greasy products are left on the outside edge of the pile. They must be buried into the compost pile and should be mixed with high-carbon materials such as sawdust, shavings, or dry leaves to prevent the odor and the waste of the nitrogen escaping from the pile. The other option is to put the animal-attracting ingredients in a metal container with a lid to break down for a while before adding them to the larger exposed pile.

Compost over Grass

Q. What do you suggest about applying compost over grass clippings on the lawn? Is there a point at which the grass clippings may be too heavy or cause problems for the turf?

A. Applying about an inch of compost in the fall is probably the very best thing you can do for the turf.

Compost Tips

Here are a couple of good tips from a reader:

Q. If bare-rooted trees are not ready to be planted, they can be kept alive for a long time by putting the roots in the finished compost pile. I have done this "heeling in" process with large plants and plants that people have dug up and put out to be taken to the landfill. Much of my landscape has come from people's trash. Also on compost, one of the best ways I have found to manage the compost is to use one section of your vegetable garden for the pile. When finished, the compost is located right where you need it. Then you move the location to another part of the garden and build the next pile. Continue this until you have covered the whole garden. The compost piles condition the soil and make it ready for productive growing.

A. Good tips, but make sure the compost has completed its active cooking or the roots of the trees will be cooked as well.

Hay in the Compost

Q. We put out some hay bales for fall decoration. I would add the hay to the compost pile, but I have heard you talk about some hay still having herbicide residue. How do I test it?

A. Grow some peanut plants in pots from raw peanuts, make a tea out of the questionable compost, and use the tea to water the plants. If the peanut leaves roll up and look wilted, don't use the hay without composting it for at least a year. Picloram and Clopyralid are the worst culprits that are sprayed on grasses to kill broad-leafed plants, but other herbicides are also resistant to breakdown.

Maggots in the Compost

Q. My compost pile is overridden with maggots. The pile was built on bare soil where a portable storage building was removed. A rat was buried beneath this area about two months prior to starting the pile. Could it be the cause of the maggots? They appear to be degrading everything that goes in the pile, but am I going to be fly infested as a result?

A. Fear not! These are the larvae of a beneficial insect called the soldier fly or black soldier fly. These leathery, segmented worms help break down the compost materials. The adult is a beneficial blue-black wasplike fly that feeds on nectar and helps pollinate flowers. If you keep the compost pile soupy wet, you might see another beneficial: the rat-tailed maggot, which grows up to be another pollinator—one of the hover flies—whose larvae feed on pest insects.

Roaches in the Compost Pile

Q. I have successfully maintained a large compost pile for more than five years with no problems. When turning the pile a couple of weeks ago, four or five large roaches scurried out and scared me to death. I hate roaches, and I sure don't want them in my compost pile. I'm treating perimeter areas of my house with boric acid. What can I do to get them out of the compost pile? I mainly fill the pile with kitchen scraps (vegetable and fruit waste, coffee grounds, eggshells), dryer lint, grass clippings, and leaves. Am I doing anything wrong?

A. Get a grip! Roaches are not only no threat outdoors and in the compost pile, they are beneficial by feeding on and helping break down organic matter. Next—boric acid should never be used outdoors because it will foul up the chemistry of the soil in a hurry. Other than that, you aren't doing anything wrong except driving yourself crazy. To make the insects less active around the compost pile, turn it more often, add dry molasses or a product that contains it, and sprinkle natural diatomaceous earth around and over the pile after turning.

COMPOST CHECKLIST

A lot of misinformation about composting exists, and most of it makes the process seem too difficult. Compost creation is more of a fact than either an art or a science. All living things—plants and animals—will die and then rot to become compost. All you have to do is make a pile of previously living materials. Nature will do the rest. It's easy, but here are some points that might help your composting seem even easier.

1. *Compost bins.* Containers really aren't necessary. Heaps or piles work just fine. Mesh, lumber, shipping pallets, cinder blocks, or hay bales can be used if space is limited. Covers aren't necessary except in monsoon weather. Compost piles can be located in the shade or in full sun.

2. *Bio-activators and other additives.* Bacteria-laden powders, liquids, and special inoculants are usually unnecessary. Every piece of organic matter is naturally covered with thousands or even millions of fungi and bacteria. Yeast, sugar, and molasses will serve as natural biostimulants if you feel it's necessary to speed up the process. Molasses is probably the best choice.

3. *Worms.* Adding earthworms or worm cocoons is unnecessary. If the dead material is piled and moisture is added, the biology of the compost pile will include earthworms. Molasses, dry or liquid, will attract earthworms better than any ingredient. It will also repel fire ants from the pile.

4. *Fertilizer.* Synthetic nitrogen fertilizers are unbalanced and harsh and contain excess mineral salts and often even contaminants. It's legal for industrial wastes to be in synthetic fertilizers. Natural fertilizers like cottonseed meal, coffee, manures, and dried blood work well. Food products like cornmeal are also beneficial in the compost blend.

5. *Lime, sulfur, calcium.* Adding calcium to raise the pH or adding iron or sulfur to lower the pH of the pile is an unnecessary waste of time. Finished compost is almost always nearly neutral. On the other hand, a very small amount of sulfur added to the pile will stimulate the feeding of the microbes and thus the heat and decomposition of the pile. But be careful. More than 1 cup of sulfur per cubic yard will actually hurt the microbes.

6. *Odors.* Stink results from too much moisture, too much nitrogen, and not enough air. Problems can result from excess grass clippings, too many food scraps, or too much manure. To reduce odors, add more carbon in the form of dry leaves or sawdust and turn the pile more often to increase the oxygen.

7. *Animals and insects.* Animals like mice and rats and insects like roaches and pillbugs can become a nuisance even though they are helping break down the organic material. Bird feed, pet food, scraps from the kitchen, and the bodies of dead animals can attract hungry animals. Just make sure to put these kinds of ingredients down into the center of the pile or in metal containers. And yes—it is okay to put the pet waste and dead animals into the compost pile. That's exactly where they should go.

8. *Layers.* Carefully placing the ingredients into lasagna-style layers looks good in the beginning, but it's a total waste of time. Just mix all the materials together. They'll be that way after the first turning anyway.

9. *Turning.* It's optional. The pile will decompose into compost without it, but stirring or turning has two advantages. The oxygen will stimulate the faster breakdown of the raw materials and the outside edge of the pile will be exposed to the microbe feeding of the interior.

10. *Carbon-to-nitrogen ratios.* This is too much science and math for me. Compost piles thrive when various amounts and various types of materials are mixed together. Ratios are fine to worry about if you don't have anything else to do, but all organic materials will compost in a timely manner if given water, air, and time.

Synthetic versus Natural Fertilizers

Organic fertilizers are significantly different from synthetic fertilizers. Synthetic fertilizers contain no organic material. They have a nitrogen-phosphorus-potassium (N-P-K) analysis such as 16-4-8 printed on the bag. That means the contents are supposed to be 16 percent nitrogen, 4 percent phosphorus, and 8 percent potassium—a total of 28 percent. The big question is: What makes up the other 72 percent of the stuff in the bag? It's labeled as "inert." In the state of Texas, fertilizer manufacturers are not required to disclose the nature of this material. It could be something innocuous like clay pellets or granulated limestone, or it could be hazardous industrial waste. There are documented examples of the latter problem.

Now you might ask, "Why do we need filler?" The manufacturers distribute the N-P-K throughout the filler or carrier so you don't burn the heck out of your turf when you apply it. Does that tell you something?

When we use organic fertilizers, we're using very low amounts of buffered nutrients. Everything in the bag is useful to the plant. Our "filler" is organic material with a variety of trace minerals. That translates into much better stimulation of biological activity in the soil.

Synthetic fertilizers are water soluble. They create high levels of salts and nitrates in the soil, which kill or repel beneficial soil organisms. Organic fertilizers are not water soluble. They will not leach out and pollute our waterways. They are 100 percent soil food, including trace minerals. They also release their nutrients slowly—at a rate that allows plants to absorb them as needed—whereas synthetic fertilizers glut plants, causing rapid but weak growth.

The most common criticism of organic fertilizers and lame support of synthetic fertilizers is that the plant can't tell the difference between synthetic and organic fertilizers. So why not save money and use the fake stuff? Also, the organic fertilizers work too slowly. That is all nonsense! Plants can indeed tell the difference. They need a balance of major nutrients and trace minerals. Synthetic fertilizers do not provide that balance. The most glaring omission is carbon. Organic fertilizers have lots of carbon in the organic matter. The high-nitrogen, salt-based synthetics have virtually none. Life can't exist without carbon.

There are all kinds of problems with synthetic high-nitrogen fertilizers. The primary issue is that there's too much nitrogen. It creates an unbalanced situation as far as nutrients in the soil and in plants. And the form of nitrogen is wrong. It works too fast. Plus, it's soluble. If it rains after you put it out it washes away and leaches through the soil into the water stream.

Yes, synthetic fertilizers grow plants quickly and appear to be helpful. The problem is that they force plants to grow in an artificially fast and unhealthy condition. The soluble high-nitrogen plant foods produce unnaturally forced growth that results in watery plant cells without the proper nutrition. All that does is invite insect pests and diseases. When plants are stressed and unhealthy, Mother Nature sends in the cleanup crews. Their mission is to take out the sick and unhealthy and improve the gene pool.

The second problem in synthetic fertilizer is the phosphorous source, which is triple superphosphate 0-46-0. Years ago, the phosphorous source was 0-20-0 superphosphate. It was pretty darn good even though it was created by a synthetic process. Rock phosphate was treated with sulfuric acid. It was a more balanced phosphate and did not tie up trace minerals.

Well, somebody came up with the notion to use phosphoric acid to create more phosphorous for less money. So now all the synthetic-fertilizer manufacturers use triple superphosphate. Big problem: The new material is so raw and so bare that when it's put on the soil, it grabs and locks onto magnesium, manganese, and all sorts of other trace minerals, tying them up and making them unavailable to plants.

The third problem is potassium. The source of potassium in most synthetic fertilizers is muriate of potash or potassium chloride. Potassium chloride is bad on specific types of crops—especially fruit crops. It's also harsh on the soil. What we like as a potassium source is potassium sulfate. It's made from the salt of the Great Salt Lake in Utah.

TYPES OF ORGANIC FERTILIZERS

My definition of a fertilizer is anything that improves the soil and helps to stimulate plant growth. For example, dead leaves that fall off a tree are fertilizers. As they break down, they turn into organic matter or humus and feed the soil microbes. Microbes such as the beneficial fungi on the roots protect and feed the root hairs of the plants. This feeding process releases the nutrients to feed plants. That's how it works on the prairie and in the forest. We're just speeding up the process.

All the basic soil amendments meet that definition, but they are intended for building beds more than for routine fertilizing. They are more gentle and work more slowly over time. The basic soil amendments are manure-based organic compost, cornmeal, lava sand, Texas greensand, zeolite, and dry molasses. These should be applied up to three times a year for the first few years of an organic program.

Manure-based compost. This is the basic building block of organics. It is the material we would find on an undisturbed forest floor. It acts as a gentle fertilizer by encouraging microbial action.

Cornmeal. This natural fungicide is a mild fertilizer and disease fighter that should be used until your soil gets healthy.

Lava sand. You can use as much as you want as long as you want. Remember that the most productive soils in the world—which come from places with a history of volcanic action: Costa

Rica, Hawaii, and parts of the West Coast and the Mediterranean—are almost solid lava.

Texas greensand. Mined from ancient sea beds, Texas greensand is loaded with iron and other trace minerals. It can be a bit of a problem in soils with high levels of iron.

Dry molasses. This is not solid dried molasses. It's organic material, like rice hull bits, that has been sprayed with molasses and dried. It is a powerful carbon source that really kicks up microbial activity.

There are many quality bagged organic fertilizers to choose from. Some people alternate among them on the perfectly logical supposition that each contains a slightly different combination of nutrients, and by rotating over time, you provide your soil a more balanced diet.

Some widely distributed brands are Alliance, GreenSense, Garden-Ville, Hu-more, Bradfield, Bluebonnet, Sustane, Bioform, and Texas Tee. Several stores carry their own brand, including Redenta's, Calloway's, and North Haven Gardens. Bagged sewer sludge, or biosolids, is another product of which I approve. In general, it is better to select one of these that is produced closer to home—both Denton and Houston produce a sludge product. Milorganite is an acceptable product, but be aware that it is shipped all the way from Milwaukee.

Similarly, there are a lot of great choices in liquid fertilizers. I strongly recommend a regular foliar-spray program. You can make your own Garrett Juice—the recipe is in the Appendix— or you can buy it commercially.

Other good choices are fish and seaweed products like Bioform, Maxicrop, Medina HastaGro, and GreenSense Foliar Juice. These function as a fertilizer in the soil as well as a foliar feed when sprayed on plant foliage.

You get indirect pest control from all liquid organic products because they stimulate biological activity. And that's how we really control pests the best. We try not to kill the bad guys, but rather to stimulate the good guys. The good guys feed on the pathogens, and the balance is brought forth that way.

But some products contain some synthetic materials. I don't have a big problem with that. You just have to understand and be honest about it. HastaGro and Bioform 8-8-8 have a little urea in the product. Bioform 4-2-4, on the other hand, is a pure organic product.

The amount of urea that you're putting on the plants when you use those products is very small. But urea used at a low level really kicks microbes in the rear and gets them going. It probably works almost as well as the molasses. Those are the products I recommend when people ask, "What's an organic equivalent to Miracle-Gro?" Medina HastaGro and Bioform 8-8-8 will perform just like the fast-acting soluble products such as Miracle-Gro, Peters 20-20-20, or one of the other liquids that are not acceptable in an organic program.

Many good organic fertilizers provide the proper balance of N-P-K, carbon, and trace minerals. Here's a rundown on some of the best and the worst.

Ammonia

Q. I have a neighbor who swears by a foliar spray of ammonia and dishwashing detergent (like Joy) in a hose-end sprayer. She claims it rids her yard of insects and fertilizes as well. They do have a nice lawn. What do you think of this?

A. Household ammonia is a very harsh, toxic, synthetic source of nitrogen, and soaps are harmful to beneficial life in the soil. Her lawn might look good now, but it won't for long.

Azalea Fertilizer

Q. Our local garden club has been using a synthetic 13-13-13 fertilizer on the azalea beds. Please advise what organic product can be used in its place?

A. Most any of the organic fertilizers will work, especially when used with compost, earthworm castings, lava sand, and Texas greensand. Building the beds in the first place with 50 percent compost and 50 percent shredded native cedar is another change I recommend over the commonly recommended peat moss and pine bark mix. It's also helpful to add 1 gallon of cornmeal, 1 gallon of Texas greensand, and 5 gallons of lava sand to the mix.

Too Much Molasses?

Q. Is it possible to use too much dry molasses?

A. Yes, too much sugar of any kind will stimulate too much microbial activity in the soil. The heat of microbe feeding generated by an excess of sugar will fry the roots of plants. I've learned this the hard way. Use dry molasses at the rate of 5–10 pounds per 1,000 square feet. It's possible to use too much of anything, organic or synthetic. Too much water can kill you. It's called drowning. Liquid molasses should be used at 1–2 ounces per gallon of water.

Which Kind of Molasses?

Q. We are preparing a bed for shrubs, grapevines, and blackberries. Is the molasses they sell in the feed store the right kind of molasses, or is it different? Also what kind of organic fertilizer should be used?

A. Any kind of molasses is useful. Sugar of any kind is a carbohydrate and food for microorganisms in the soil. Molasses is better, and dark blackstrap molasses is the best because it contains so many trace minerals, including iron and sulfur. Molasses can be used in many ways. It can be mixed with biological insecticides such as Bio-Worm or other Bt products to make them last longer. It can be put into a water spray prior to ladybug releases to encourage these helpful insects, which will be thirsty when first released, and they seem to have a sweet tooth. It can be added to the irrigation water to supply trace minerals and stimulate soil organisms. It is an important ingredient in the Garrett Juice mix. For these liquid uses, add ½ to 1 ounce per gallon of water. Use dry molasses at 5 pounds per 1,000 square feet. My most common recommendation for the first application when converting from toxic chemicals to the Natural Way is to apply the dry molasses. This approach has been used on several sports fields with great success. It is cost effective and productive.

Manure

Q. Our soil here is very hard clay. Our house is on high ground. We are planting some Bradford pears. We had holes dug by a backhoe. Today I got some old, dry, flaky cow manure from our neighbor's barn. I layered the bottom of the hole with manure, then added a layer of dirt, repeating these layers to near the top. Late this evening, after I completed the planting, my wife said that you cannot do this because when the roots hit the manure they will burn. Is this true? Am I going to have to dig the holes back out? The trees are about 6 feet tall.

A. Burn is just one of the possible problems caused by burying organic matter. It will also create anaerobic gases because of the lack of oxygen in the bottom of the hole. It will also make it very difficult to balance the watering. The manures, mulches, and other organic amendments should only be used on the surface of the soil after you have backfilled with nothing but native soil and settled it with water. Sorry—your wife is right.

Miracle-Gro Alternatives

Q. I have planted my first perennial flower bed, and everyone recommends Miracle-Gro. Please repeat the information from your show yesterday about forcing flowers with organic products.

A. You don't have to use the high-nitrogen soluble fertilizers to get excellent flower production. Fast-acting organic fertilizers that contain small amounts of feed-grade urea include products like Organic Advantage, Medina HastaGro, and Bioform 8-8-8. They feed your plants naturally and contain the all-important trace minerals, including carbon. The secret is to get the soil and the roots of the plants healthy enough so that the natural feeding of soil microbes provides the fertility. The blue-green soluble products feed the plants hydroponically. Your flower production will be great and longer lasting if you use plenty of compost, earthworm castings, lava sand, Texas greensand, and cornmeal in the potting soil or bedding soil. Use a Garrett Juice or fish and seaweed foliar feeding about once every two weeks. Mulching with pure shredded cedar will also help. Advantages of this approach include less cost each year, more production each year, and beds that never have to be removed or replaced, as they would with the synthetic fertilizers.

Rabbit Pellets

Q. The people who just moved out of our rental house left a pile of rabbit droppings where they had a rabbit hutch. I assume that this can be used as fertilizer. How do I use it? Would it be useful in my compost pile?

A. Rabbit manure is one of the best natural fertilizers in the world and can be used directly in the garden soil or in the compost pile first. Since it is naturally buffered, I would save the time and use it directly in the beds at about 20–40 pounds per 1,000 square feet.

Root Stimulators

Q. Should root stimulators be used on newly planted trees?

A. Yes, if you use the right ones. Commonly recommended root stimulators are basically synthetic fertilizers with very high amounts of phosphorous. Confusing recommendations are given out by the organiphobes, who also say not to use high-phosphorous fertilizers in general. They recommend the 3-1-2 ratio fertilizers for general use, but then when they talk about planting trees and other new plants, they recommend these root stimulators that have very high phosphorous levels like 5-20-10. Both are bad recommendations because neither of these fertilizers is balanced. Neither contains any carbon or organic matter, and nothing in nature has such a dramatic range or such high levels of nitrogen, phosphorus, and potassium.

Good, gentle, natural root stimulators include compost tea, Garrett Juice, seaweed tea, weed tea, or alfalfa tea. Never heard of weed tea? Just soak a bunch of fresh green weeds in water. Just as when making compost tea, fill the container half full of weeds, cover and fill to the top with water, and use after 3–10 days.

Sludge, or Biosolids

Q. What do you think about the Milorganite fertilizer?

A. Human-sludge fertilizers are good if the heavy metal and

pesticide tests and prevention are done on a continuing basis. And they are. No other fertilizer has this intensive degree of testing and inspection. Eliminating the toxic poisons from the market is the way to end that worry. I don't see the point, however, of using Milwaukee sludge when we have our own right here in Texas— Hou-Actinite in Houston, Dillo Dirt in Austin, and Dino Soil in Denton. Biosolids, which are well-composted sludge, are included in several of the Garden-Ville fertilizers and in the Sick Tree Treatment product.

Iron Supplementation

Q. Is there a natural source of iron available to put in my yard and plants? I have a fair amount of yellow in my grass, plants, and trees. I've been 100 percent organic for about four years. What else can I do?

A. Yes, Texas greensand. It not only has 14–20 percent iron but also lots of trace minerals. Several brand names are available, and the greensand should be applied at about 40–80 pounds per 1,000 square feet or 4–8 pounds per 100 square feet. As has been reported, some of the commercial iron products contain significant amounts of arsenic and lead—especially Ironite. Another excellent natural iron-containing product is Earth's Fortune.

Foliar-Feeding

Q. Do I need to continue foliar-feeding my shrubs and perennials through the fall and winter?

A. No, spray only the cool-season plants that are still growing—pansies, Johnny-jump-ups, fescue, rye, and others. The organic spray won't hurt anything on dormant plants and certainly will benefit the soil, but it's probably not worth the time and expense to use on those plants.

Zeolite

Zeolite is a natural volcanic mineral. It contains a wide array of basic minerals that were spewed back to the earth's surface in a cataclysmic event—a volcanic eruption. Over millions of years, hot springs leached the calcium, sodium, and other contaminants out, leaving a unique material.

Finely ground zeolite has an amazing capacity to grab things—all kinds of odors in the air and contaminants in the soil. It especially likes ammonia—raw nitrogen. So, if you've been using synthetic fertilizer, an application of zeolite will grab that excess nitrogen and release it slowly so it is useful to plants—*and* so it isn't leached into our water systems.

Zeolite's capacity to grab odors makes it a great material in cat litter. And it's the crunchy material that comes in those little bags that are sold to absorb odors in refrigerators, closets, and such.

It's also reusable. I bought a chunk of it at an aquarium shop. I keep it in my aquarium with my albino frogs. Periodically, I put it out in the yard in the fresh air and sunshine, where it releases the absorbed odors. Then I put it back with the frogs. This is a very useful product in the organic program.

The recommended organic fertilization program:
First fertilization—As early as January on into March
Second fertilization—Sometime in June
Third fertilization—Between September and October

Pest Control and Beneficial Insects

The most common cause of insect and disease pests on plants is the use of large amounts of synthetic fertilizers. When synthetic high-nitrogen fertilizer is used, plants absorb too much nitrogen in relation to other nutrients. To prevent the nitrogen buildup from becoming toxic, plants must grow fast. To do this, the lignin of the cell walls is much thinner than normal. Cells are also more watery. Unlike humans, most insects see in the ultraviolet portion of the sunlight spectrum. Insects can detect this reflection difference between healthy and unhealthy cells in plants. Since healthy lignin is a very tough substance and difficult for insects to chew through, the weak cells produce a reflectivity that is like a neon sign flashing "Come Eat at Joe's."

So, keeping the soil healthy and the plants stress free is the basis of organic pest control. On the other hand, when pests occasionally pop up, mild organic products are available, and they are effective.

ALTHEA RUST

Q. What can I do about rust on altheas? I have a hedge of eight of them. The county extension agent diagnosed the rust and recommended Funginex. It did not work, and the smell scared me.

A. Funginex would be a poor recommendation even if it worked. It's a synthetic neurotoxin, and the natural products work better. Rust is a fungal disease that can be controlled with nontoxic tools. Apply horticultural cornmeal to the soil at 10–20 pounds per 1,000 square feet, and for even more control, use the entire Sick Tree Treatment. In late winter when the buds start to swell, but before bud break, spray the plants and the soil around the plants with Garrett Juice plus one of the following: baking soda at 1 rounded tablespoon per gallon, potassium bicarbonate at the same rate, or skim milk at 1 cup per gallon.

ANTS

Q. I am having a problem with ants eating my okra. They are on no other plants in my garden. The remainder of the garden is fine. I have sprayed garlic-pepper tea and dusted them with all-purpose flour. Neither has helped. Any suggestions?

A. Fire ants, which are the only ants that eat okra, can be controlled by spraying Garden-Ville Auntie Fuego or GreenSense Soil Drench. You can make your own citrus spray by combining 2 ounces of orange oil concentrate or d-limonene with 2 ounces of molasses and a cup of compost tea per gallon of water. Neem products will also help keep ants off plants.

Carpenter Ants in Trees

Q. This past summer a dear computer buddy visited me and got me to pay attention to my outdoors. I am astounded. Was it this much fun all the time and I was just too stupid to realize it? I do have one problem. I have carpenter ants. They are chewing up this wonderful old tree I have in the back yard, and I think they are attacking one of my wooden fences. I read up on the Internet various chemical ways to attack them, but I wanted to ask you for some kind of organic way to attack these little buggers and save my tree.

A. Welcome aboard! Actually it gets easier and more fun the more you plant and the more you learn from personal experiences. There are no major universities teaching the organic techniques, so we have to learn by talking with other gardeners, reading, and experimenting. I discover something new every week and have changed my recommendations significantly since starting to learn the Natural Way in the late 1980s. Changes and updates will no doubt continue into the 2000s. If you discover something that works well, let us know and we'll pass it on.

The carpenter ants are not hurting your tree. They only infest dead and decaying wood. Something else has caused the damage to the tree. Clean out the dead stuff, but be careful not to injure any living tissue or the disease will spread farther into the tree. Spray or splash hydrogen peroxide on the opening, but don't fill the cavity or paint it with wound dressing. Apply the Sick Tree Treatment to the soil, and the chances are good that the tree will live a while longer. The carpenter ants are only a problem if they decide to go into your house and dig out the walls. There they can be controlled with any of the boric acid products indoors or the citrus-oil products outdoors. Boric acid will damage the soil.

APHIDS AND OTHER SMALL INSECTS

Insect pests aren't the main problem, only a symptom. The solution is to build soil health for long-lasting control. For short-term control, spray products that contain seaweed, and release ladybugs, green lacewings, and trichogramma wasps. Spray garlic tea as a preventative. Spray garlic-pepper tea or Garrett Juice plus citrus oil if needed. Spray foliage with molasses and water before releasing beneficial insects. A strong blast of water will rip most aphids from the leaves and kill them. Aphids usually feed on the new foliage of plants in the early spring and stressed foliage in the fall. Both are normally temporary problems.

Tip from a Reader

I wanted to let you know what has worked for me to get the aphids off my two hibiscus trees. I peel two garlic cloves, cut them in half, and place the halves in the pot just below the soil level, about 2 inches from the stem. Push in with your finger. Water. Within twenty-four hours the aphids are gone! They hate the garlic. It works perfect every time and lasts up to four months.

ARMYWORMS

Q. We have small green-and-black-striped worms that are killing our Bermudagrass. So far, there has been no damage to the zoysia. What can we do to get rid of them without harm to our dogs? The worms are also in our swimming pool.

A. Well, there finally is an advantage of zoysia. Spray the Bt as a last resort, since it will kill other moth and butterfly larvae. Those are armyworms, and they can be controlled easily with any of the citrus-based sprays or Bt (*Bacillus thuringiensis*) products. Add 1 ounce of molasses per gallon for greater control.

BAGWORMS AND CATERPILLARS

Release trichogramma wasps. Spray *Bacillus thuringiensis* (Bt) products or spray Garrett Juice plus garlic. The ultimate weapon is the fire ant control formula. Commercial products include Garden-Ville Auntie Fuego and GreenSense Soil Drench.

BEES

I got this question from a beekeeper. It seems that one of the biggest problems beekeepers face in keeping their bees alive is a *Nosema* disease. Is the *Nosema* bait for grasshoppers dangerous for bees? No, *Nosema apis* is the disease that will kill honeybees, and *Nosema bombi* kills bumblebees. But the product we've been recommending contains *Nosema locustae*, which is a different species and will not affect our helpful bees.

Q. Our area seems to be devoid of any bees, wasps, or hornets this year. I haven't heard anything about this phenomenon. Any ideas?

A. The pesticides have just about wiped them out in many areas of Texas and other states. This is a key reason we all need to be organic. One of the worst culprits is a pesticide that has the unfounded reputation of being mildly toxic. The common name is Sevin, the chemical is carbaryl, and it's in the carbamate class of chemicals. It is a highly toxic insecticide— especially to bees. That's why it says that in large black letters on the label. All you can do is be organic and try to convince your neighbors to do the same. Also, plant as many flowering plants as you can. Be careful to include plants that flower in various seasons and to use many different colors.

BENEFICIAL INSECTS

Don't fall into the trap of thinking that the mild weather will mean more pest bugs. If good weather helps the population of pest bugs, it will also help the beneficials. The balance would also remain if the winter was severe. Furthermore, most insects are beneficial. Even some of the troublesome insects like aphids perform beneficial services. The goal is to establish a natural balance. There are three beneficial insects that I want you to buy and release starting in the early spring: trichogramma wasps, green lacewings, and lady beetles or ladybugs. Trichogramma wasps are tiny gnatlike wasps that are very effective in controlling pecan casebearers, loopers, greenworms, and other small caterpillars. They are parasites, not predators. They are released by simply pinning the 1-inch-square cards in trees or on wood stakes in the garden. Green lacewings are pretty little flies with large wings. Their larvae love to eat aphids, red spider mites, lacebugs, thrips, and many other pest bugs. Trichogramma wasps and lacewings are both released in egg form when plants first leaf out. The adult ladybugs are released directly on aphid-infested plants after giving the plants a blast of water from the garden hose— or in the morning when the dew is on the foliage. These beneficials, along with more detailed release information, are available at the ever increasing number of organic garden centers and feed stores.

BORERS IN TREES

Q. I am experiencing a bad infestation of borers in some of my eldarica pines. What do you recommend for this problem?

A. Apply beneficial nematodes to the holes in the trunk and to the soil in the root zone. Next, apply the Sick Tree Treatment. Avoid the toxic chemical poisons— they treat symptoms only, don't solve the problems, and waste money. By the way, some of the so-called experts recommend wrapping the trunks of trees. That is the most foolish thing of all to do. Not only will it not prevent borers, it gives the insects a nice place to hide out and actually encourages them. What really controls borers is healthy trees.

BOXELDER BUGS

Q. I have what I think are called boxelder bugs infesting my detached garage/workshop/barn. They are a dark charcoal gray with red on the back. They do not appear harmful, but they are a nuisance. The problem is they are pests. They are thick on the outside walls of the barn, and they come inside and die. I also do not like them falling down the back of my shirt while I am using my table saw! I was using Dursban in the past, but now I realize I was simply raising a herd of Dursban-resistant bugs. Are they harmful to a food crop when/if I ever get a garden started? What do they feed on? All I have in the area are the pear trees and Bermudagrass.

A. Boxelder bugs primarily eat tree seeds, and you are right— they are mostly a nuisance. Check them out in the *Texas Bug Book,* and spray with one of the citrus-based products or with neem if you decide to kill them. Dusting them with cinnamon will also make them move along. Mix the cinnamon with natural diatomaceous earth for a more economical mixture.

BROWN RECLUSE SPIDERS

Q. We're having a problem with brown recluse spiders in our house, and my husband was bitten by one last week. We need to know what steps you would take to eliminate this problem.

A. The citrus products like Orange Guard will kill those guys just as well as any of the toxic chemicals but will not contaminate the house. If you like to make your own mixes, use 1 ounce of orange oil or a d-limonene product like Orange TKO per quart of water. This mixture is also an excellent cleaner.

BUTTERFLIES

Q. Your advice to use Nolo Bait and neem-oil spray saved our baby pecan trees from nasty grasshoppers. Thank you so very much. I raise Monarch and Painted Lady butterflies in an outdoor tent on milkweed plants. What can I use to control plant pests that will not harm eggs, larvae, or adult butterflies? Your book says to use liquid seaweed, citrus oil, and soapy water for various pests. Will any of these remedies hurt the ova, larvae, or adult butterflies? Adult butterflies feed on nectar and artificial nectar that I make. I work with about two hundred other butterfly breeders who would also like to have the remedy to these insects in their raising tents.

A. Citrus and soap will hurt the other life cycles of the butterflies. Seaweed alone or the Garrett Juice mixture will not. The best approach is to use biological control—ladybugs, green lacewings, and beneficial nematodes.

CHIGGERS

Q. One of our Eagle Scout candidates wishes to make an outdoor area at our church for worship services. It is currently infested with chiggers. The land surrounding this area includes several acres that our church will eventually build on, but this picnic area will remain. Do you have any ideas what we could use to treat this large area without chemicals to help solve this problem? We can't even put up a backstop because of this problem. The land is covered with high grass and mesquite trees.

A. The solution for chiggers in the black and white soils of North Texas is also an important step in building the soil health. Start by mowing the area, as chiggers like the tall grass. Broadcast elemental sulfur at 5 pounds per 1,000 square feet and dry molasses at 10 pounds. This procedure will help balance the soil chemistry, stimulate the beneficial microorganisms, and control the critters. If the budget allows, broadcast humate at 10 pounds per 1,000 square feet and dry molasses at 5 pounds per 1,000 square feet.

CHINCH BUGS

Dust problem area with natural diatomaceous earth after spraying with Garrett Juice (compost tea, molasses, seaweed, apple cider vinegar,) and 2 ounces of orange oil per gallon of water. Water and fertilize a little more carefully. Chinch bugs are a sign of severe turf stress.

CRICKETS

Treat problem areas with *Nosema locustae* products. Spray Garrett Juice plus garlic. Any of the orange-oil-based products will kill crickets effectively on contact.

CUTWORMS

Q. While dividing my dianthus, I discovered large, mature cutworms. They were directly underneath each clump. Diatomaceous earth does not seem to be doing the trick. Neither did Dipel. What would you recommend using to save my perennials? Would beneficial nematodes be effective? If so, would the soil have to be free of any other form of insecticide, such as a systemic like Orthene, for a certain amount of time? I keep my yard immaculate and dispose of weeds and garden debris. I do not want to resort to harmful pesticides.

A. Use the fire ant control solution and follow with a release of beneficial nematodes. The cutworms will be history. Stop throwing away weeds and other organic debris. At least put them in the compost pile. Building the organic matter and thus the carbon in the soil is the long-term solution to almost all pest problems. Use the same drench as mentioned above for any existing contaminants.

FIRE ANTS

Fire ant problems are human-made— self-inflicted. When fire ants landed in Alabama some fifty-odd years ago, there was only one queen per mound, and the colonies were territorial. Only dozens of mounds per acre was the norm. After the infested areas were doused and sprayed with malathion, Dursban, diazinon, Orthene, and Myrex, the ants adapted. Now there are hundreds or even thousands of queens per mound and many thousands of mounds per acre. The only solution is the organic approach.

Drench problem mounds with a mix of any product made of orange oil, compost tea, and molasses. To make the concentrate, use one part compost tea, one part molasses, and one part orange oil or d-limonene. Then use 4 – 6 ounces of the mix per gallon of water for treating fire ant mounds. Commercial products include Garden-Ville Auntie Fuego, Garden-Ville Soil Conditioner, and GreenSense Soil Drench. Next, treat the site with beneficial nematodes. These are living organisms and must be used before the date deadline on the package. The last and most important step is to go organic. The biodiversity of microbes, insects, and other animals is the best long-term control of fire ants. Spraying the site regularly with an organic spray that contains molasses will also help. Fire ants hate molasses. Synthetic chemical baits and contact poisons are unnecessary and don't work anyway. If the toxins did work, why do we still have so many fire ants?

Q. I have fire ants, and I will not use poison or gasoline to kill them. I mix cornmeal and boric acid, put it on the mounds and leave it in small clumps, and the ants come get it. Dampen the cornmeal slightly so the boric acid will stick to it. For some reason, fire ants love cornmeal. I guess they take it to the queen because within two days the whole mound is dead! I tried mixing sugar with boric acid, but the ants like the cornmeal better.

A. Thanks for the report. The only problem I have with your technique is that— yes, the soil needs boron, but very little. Boron toxicity can easily occur unless the boric acid is used in very small amounts.

Three-Step Fire Ant Program

1. Drench the mounds with Garden-Ville Auntie Fuego, GreenSense Soil Drench, or similar compost tea, molasses, and orange oil product.
2. Apply beneficial nematodes.
3. Go totally organic.

Listener Tip

I have no proof that this works, but several listeners have reported that an application of the Alliance Soil Amendment has somehow caused the fire ants to vanish. No downside in trying that.

FIREFLIES

Q. Where can I buy firefly larvae?

A. I don't know any insectaries that have the wonderful fireflies, but all you have to do is go totally organic and they will return. We have had them on our property for the last several years. Besides being beautiful, they are highly beneficial. Fireflies' larvae have a favorite food— baby slugs and snails.

FLEAS

Q. I like to use nontoxic, natural methods where I can, but I do have two items that you are addressing which concern me. (1) You have said more than once that modern pesticides don't work on flea control because the mature fleas are not in the yard/home/garage, etc., but are only on the animals. This is just not true. Fleas do, of course, inhabit the host animal, but not exclusively. They may be found in abundance in lawns and homes from which the host animal has long been absent, and when you walk in, the dinner bell rings. (2) The warnings on the neem package really sound scary. Is it a dangerous product?

A. You are right about fleas except for one thing. The only fleas on the site are nonadults— eggs, larvae, and pupae. The adults are on the animals. Therefore, applying pesticides to the site kills no fleas but does contaminate the site. What you witness when walking across the lawn is pupae literally exploding into adults in the presence of warmth and carbon dioxide coming from your body or the pets. Beneficial nematodes applied to the site and bathing dogs with herbal shampoos that contain d-limonene (citrus oil) is by far the most effective treatment and best value in flea and tick control. Unfortunately, some cats' skin is very sensitive to the orange oil. For them, just use other mild herbal shampoos that do not contain d-limonene.

The scary-sounding warnings on the neem label are typical insecticide boiler plate. Neem is a very safe and effective natural pest control. It is made from the seed of a tropical tree, *Azadirachta indica*. Although it is an excellent insect- and disease-control product for plants, it is also used in toothpastes, skin creams, and other human products. There's a good little book that will give you all the details: *Neem: A Tree for Solving Global Problems* (Washington, D.C.: National Academy Press, 1992).

FLIES

Q. I have a problem with houseflies. They are accumulating in my garage (hundreds of them)! I have a makeshift greenhouse on the patio near my garage, and two doors down my neighbor has hunting dogs in his back yard. Could either be the cause of my problem? I have washed down my crowded garage with bleach and disinfectant, but it hasn't helped!

A. Stop using bleach and disinfectants. Besides being toxic, they are unnecessary. Use orange-oil-based products such as Orange TKO or Citrus Magic for the cleaning and ask your neighbors to add natural diatomaceous earth (2 percent of the volume of the food) to their dogs' food daily. The Muenster Natural dog food is the only product that contains the proper amount of DE. Spraying the air with the same orange oil will work well on the flies in the air, as will the citronella sprays such as Skeeter D'Feeter. Garlic-pepper-tea spray will also help repel the flies.

FOREST TENT CATERPILLARS

Q. Help! I have a beautiful red oak tree that has been invaded by a fuzzy caterpillar. They are gathered in bunches of 100 or more and can be described as 1 inch long, gray and brown in color, with tiny yellow teardrop markings from front to back along the back.

A. These are forest tent caterpillars. They are common on oaks, especially in the spring. If they are severe, spray with any citrus-based product— at the most. They usually only do cosmetic damage. A strong blast of water may be enough. Make a note in your calendar to release trichogramma wasps next April 1. These tiny parasites will control this moth larvae and other caterpillars, worms, and loopers.

GRASSHOPPERS

Q. The grasshoppers have enjoyed our holly bushes immensely the past two years. They've come back strong this year, and I would like to know what to treat them with to alienate the grasshoppers or at least keep them from completely destroying the bushes.

A. Not much worked very well last year, organic or chemical, at least as far as direct sprays or dusting applications. On the other hand, some folks had little to no problems with these ravenous beasts. For example, I found one grasshopper in my garden all season, and it was sick. Without question, we know that grasshoppers are attacked and killed by beneficial organisms in the soil. For that to happen, the soil must be moist and healthy— often a difficult task in a drought summer. Here's a review of reports about successful grasshopper control in 1999.

1. The most common successful report came from those who had strong biodiversity and soil moisture. They had heavy property-line plantings, no herbicide spraying of fence lines, as well as lots of different plants inside the property. Some gardeners used

hedgerows and other mass plantings, but all had many varieties of plants blooming at different seasons. They also fed the birds heavily on a regular basis and kept the life in the garden plentiful.

2. One gardener reported no grasshopper damage after fertilizing with nothing but kelp meal— three times during the growing season. This report indicated that the adjacent neighbors had severe grasshopper damage.

3. Another gardener reported no grasshopper attacks after spreading lava sand heavily over the entire property at about ¼ inch. Again, this respondent reported no grasshoppers on her property but heavy munchinations across the fence.

4. Nolo Bait or other *Nosema locustae* products worked in several cases, but this approach offers no protection from the airborne masses of adult grasshoppers that descend and devour quickly. It does work on the nymphs as they emerge in the spring.

5. Several reports have come in about success eliminating grasshoppers by applying sulfur or sul-po-mag (k-mag). Apparently the sulfur has some significant effect.

One of the great advantages of any of these new remedies is that even if they don't control the insects, they will have improved the soil greatly. There is now a new tool called kaolin clay. It can be purchased generically or as an EPA-registered pesticide under the name Surround WP.

GRUBWORMS

Organic gardeners usually don't have grubworm problems, but beneficial nematodes are effective if they do. Maintaining healthy soil biology is the primary control. It also helps to apply sugar or dry molasses to problem areas at 5 pounds per 1,000 square feet.

Q. I know there are different kinds of grubworms. How do you get rid of the bad ones? And how do you tell the difference?

A. Only about 10 percent of the grubs in Texas soils are harmful by chewing on plant roots. The other 90 percent are beneficial because they feed on decaying organic matter. The grubs in beds are usually the good guys, but if the turf is coming loose because the roots have been eaten away, treat the soil with beneficial ne-matodes. This can be done on a preventative basis, because the same organisms also help to control fire ants, termites, fleas, ticks, and other insect pests that have at least one of their life cycles in the soil. Organic gardeners rarely have destructive levels of grub-worms because of the high level of microbiotic activity in the soil.

HOUSE PESTS

Q. When my house was built last year, skinny tubes were in-stalled in all of the walls. There are two access panels, one on each side of my house. A pest control service can pump poison into these tubes. I would like to utilize these tubes with an organic pest control service.

A. Sorry—none of the organic pesticides put out toxic fumes. Filling the tubes with a boric acid bait might work if the insects have access to it. If not, you have to treat bare wood and wall voids with boric acid or hot pepper products. An EPA-registered biolog-ical product called Bio-Blast is now available to the pest control op-erators. Spraying the insects directly with citrus-based products will kill them instantly. Orange Guard is an EPA-registered product for interior use.

Q. My husband and I will be moving into our new home this weekend. I am concerned for my family's health and well-being and would like to garden and do pest control the Natural Way. Our home is on two acres and has an aerobic septic system. Is there anything special I need to do to the land, since chlorinated water will be pumped out of the system?

A. Anything you add to the system could foul up its biological activity, but spraying a mixture of Garrett Juice plus Medina Soil Ac-tivator or any other biological stimulator onto the soil on a weekly basis won't hurt the system but will help to neutralize and dissipate the chlorine compounds in the soil and on plants. A small amount of orange oil (d-limonene), about ½ ounce (1 tablespoon per gal-lon), will also help to detoxify the contaminants. The overall or-ganic program will give you ongoing buffering of the chemicals being sprayed on the soil.

Q. What can I use in my kitchen pantry to keep moths and bugs out of dry ingredients? They ruin everything. Just today I had to throw away all of my cake mixes, dry soups, etc. I'd appreciate your input.

A. You can freeze packages two days before putting them in the pantry to kill any eggs, larvae, or pupae they may contain. Also, place packages in sealed containers. Herbs that help repel pantry moths include wormwood, sage, and bay.

MEALYBUGS

Q. What is the most effective way of ridding indoor tropical plants of mealybugs? I have been using only horticultural soap, and though it keeps them from getting worse, it doesn't seem to be killing them or making them set up home elsewhere.

A. Like aphids, mealybugs are a sure sign of plant stress. On indoor plants, that usually results from too much water, too much fertilizer, and not enough light. Therefore, the solution is to increase the light, reduce the watering schedule, and change the fertilizer program to one application a year of gentle organic products. What I like best is to use earthworm castings and lava sand. Here's another tip. Sometimes, because of the environmental stresses, the roots of plants will have fungal diseases working on them. Apply horticultural cornmeal to the surface of the soil at about ½ cup per square foot and water in. You might see the plant get healthier and kick the insect pests off quickly.

MOLES

Q. I would like to know how to get rid of moles. I know that you must get rid of the grubs, but what is the sure way to alleviate this nuisance? Can you put anything down now to kill the grubs? I have tried pellets and gas bombs on the moles, but they keep coming back. Help!

A. I bet your place glows in the dark! Let me suggest a little safer and more effective approach. Moles eat a lot more animals than just grubs, so controlling grubworms won't eliminate the problem. If you do have a harmful grub infestation, treat the soil with beneficial nematodes. They control the root-eating grubs but won't harm the beneficial organic-matter-eating grubs. The best control for moles is soil treatment with hot pepper products and castor oil. My garlic-pepper formula plus 2 ounces of castor oil per gallon works well. Mechanical devices that rattle or vibrate every few minutes are also effective.

MOSQUITOES

Mosquitoes can ruin the enjoyment of the garden, especially for women. Yes, they do bother women more than men—sugar and spice and all that. Mosquitoes have a sweet tooth. Men, women, boys, and girls who eat a lot of sugar or artificial sweeteners have more trouble with mosquitoes, and people who eat a lot of garlic seem to have fewer problems with this insect's attacks. Anyway, they can be controlled with natural techniques. Drain all stagnant water. In water that can't be drained, use *Bacillus thuringiensis* 'Israelensis' for the larvae in standing water. Mosquito-eating fish such as gambusia and other predators such as bats, purple martins, hummingbirds, damselflies, aquatic beetles, spiders, predatory mites, and dragonflies are also helpful. Spray garlic-pepper tea or orange oil products for the adults. Another solution for mosquito problems is a spray of Garrett Juice plus citrus oil. Citronella spray can also help. A commercial product is Skeeter D'Feeter. Use a very diluted solution of essential oil of lavender to mask the human odors that attract mosquitoes. Avon Skin-So-Soft and other herbal repellents also work. Lavender and eucalyptus can be sprayed or applied to the skin. Other good commercial products include Cactus Juice, LiceBGone, and Cedar-Cide.

P.S. Spraying the air with toxic chemicals such as synthetic pyrethroids is toxic, dangerous, and ineffective.

Tip from a Reader

Scientists led by Padma Vesudevan of the Indian Institute of Technology in New Delhi have determined that peppermint oil can repel mosquitoes and kill the larvae. They floated films of the oil, extracted from the peppermint plant *Mentha piperita,* on top of larvae-filled water; a day later nearly all the larvae were killed. This report was sent along with the following testing of the idea. Peppermint oil is by far the best mosquito repellent I have used. The essential oil is very strong, so we diluted it in half with witch hazel, but it lost some of its effectiveness. We then diluted it one-third with witch hazel. It worked great, and everyone smells sweet.

Footnote: I don't recommend spraying soaps that often but based on this peppermint information, Dr. Bronner's Peppermint Soap may be a good addition to mosquito sprays. Try it at 1 tablespoon per gallon. Catnip rubbed on the skin or turned into a spray has shown good results.

NEMATODES

Nematodes—good or bad? Well, some are harmful and some are beneficial. Of all the many species, root knot nematodes are the most infamous. They are parasitic and form masses of knots that deform roots of food crops and ornamental plants. Plants attacked by these bad nematodes include okra, tomatoes, eggplant, peppers, and other vegetable and ornamental crops. Other harmful nematodes cause no root knots but do cause injury by burrowing into roots, causing decay that reduces the mass and health of roots. Roots may be distorted or have swollen areas. Some nematodes cause excessive branching of roots. Some species move from plant to plant in water or on garden tools. Others attach themselves permanently to one root. Carrots and other root crop plants will be stunted with yellowed distorted leaves. Legumes such as clover, vetch, beans, and peas are supposed to have root swellings that are caused by nitrogen-fixing bacteria. The difference is that the bacteria nodules are attached to the outside of the roots. Nematodes will swell the roots from the inside.

All of the harmful nematodes are caused by plant stress and lack of biological activity in the soil. Increasing that activity is the solution. One of the fastest methods of eliminating them is to till orange- or grapefruit-peeling pulp into the soil prior to planting susceptible plants. I keep the rinds frozen in plastic bags and grind the frozen peeling into pulp for use at planting time.

Beneficial nematodes, on the other hand, are good guys. They don't eat or disturb plants in any way. Just the opposite. They eat meat—the eggs, larvae, and pupae of insects that have one of their life cycles in the ground, including fleas, grubs, flies, termites, and fire ants. Certain species such as *Heterohabditis* (Heteros) are best for the control of grubs. *Steinernema* (Steiners) seem to work best for lepidopterous insects such as moths and cutworms, and other species are the best for termites and fire ants. However, any of the beneficial species will help with the overall biological balance, resulting in the natural control of most soilborne pests.

These microscopic worms are totally harmless to people, animals, beneficial insects, and plants. They are present naturally in healthy soil. But if your population is not sufficient, you can purchase them at organic suppliers, where you'll find them in a refrigerator.

Beneficial nematodes are sensitive to heat and light. It is best to purchase them on a cool day, put them in your refrigerator, and then apply them in the cool of the evening. The best time is right before or after a rain, or after you have watered your turf. Follow the directions on the package. This is the only place where you might use a hose-end sprayer. Remove the filter. I simply dump mine in a big watering can and splash them around my yard.

POWDERY MILDEW ON CRAPE MYRTLES

Q. Three of my crape myrtles have powdery mildew, and I can't remember what to do to get rid of it.

A. Treat the soil with horticultural cornmeal at 2 pounds per 100 square feet and spray the foliage with Garrett Juice plus potassium bicarbonate at 1 rounded tablespoon per gallon of spray. Adding ½ cup milk per gallon of spray will also help.

RHINO BEETLES

Q. I recently loaded two wheelbarrows full of compost from my compost pile to use in my flower beds. I noticed several LARGE grubworms— the biggest I've ever seen. I did not put them in my flower bed but wondered what I should do with them.

A. Those grubs that are the size of your thumb are the larvae of the giant Hercules beetle or rhinoceros beetle. They are highly beneficial in that they help aerate the soil and help break down organic matter. As a matter of fact, 90 percent of all the grubs in the soil are beneficial in the same way. Only about 10 percent of the beetle grubs eat plant roots and should be considered pests. The bad grubs can be controlled by using the organic amendments to stimulate biodiverse soil health. The big guys should be protected.

ROACHES

Q. I'm having a problem with cockroaches in my compost pile. I read on your web site that you can use boric acid in your home to get rid of the pests, but I was wondering if that will work in my compost pile. I don't want to kill off my "good bugs" or make the compost useless with commercial pesticide sprays.

A. The roaches are good bugs in the compost pile. They are helping to break down organic matter. Boric acid in the compost pile is a bad idea. Boron is a very important trace mineral in the soil that helps with disease control and the taste of food products, but it doesn't take much boron to reach a toxic level. I don't recommend that any boric acid products be used outdoors—only indoors and in a limited way there.

SCALE

Q. I have recently become the environmental chairperson for my daughter's school's PTA. Last year the person in charge had control of the children's gardens. In a letter to me she wrote that "the holly bushes in the fifth-grade garden have had little white spots (Chinese wax scale). Treat by spraying Ortho Orthene sys-

temic insect control, diazinon, or malathion." Could you help me
with this and tell me a natural way to get rid of the pests?

A. What a lovely recommendation! Horticultural oil, neem, or
orange oil products will kill the pests, but unless the real problem
is solved, the pests will be back. The real problem will be something like too much or too little water, too much synthetic fertilizer, poor drainage, herbicide damage, too much or too little
shade, etc. The recommendation to use synthetic neurotoxins like
Orthene, diazinon, and malathion is not only irresponsible but
recklessly liable. All those neurotoxins are on the EPA chopping
block. Upcoming lawsuits related to these contaminants will make
the tobacco affair look like child's play. The most difficult question
for the defendants in these trials to answer will be this: Didn't you
ever listen to or read the Dirt Doctor? Food products like garlic,
pepper, cinnamon, diatomaceous earth, and citrus would control
the pests without harming the soil, air, water, pets, livestock, and
people.

SCORPIONS

Q. What do you recommend for scorpions? I was recently
stung by a scorpion in my bed, and that was the third sting this
year! Additionally, if you have any organic methods for controlling
spiders indoors, please help. We built a beautiful home in the country and can't enjoy living here due to the spiders and scorpions.

A. Scorpions are hunters. They are in and around the house
looking for juicy bugs to eat, so step one is to do a good job of the
general pest control. The bugs and the scorpions can be killed with
citrus-based sprays, diatomaceous earth, or pyrethrum products.
Pyrethrum products are organic, but because of their strong toxicity, they are among my least favorite choices. Use only natural
pyrethrum, never any products that contain PBO (piperonyl butoxide), which is a chemical synergist that negatively effects the
liver. Also, avoid the "synthetic pyrethroids." They are the next
toxic chemicals to be removed from the consumer market, right after the demise of Dursban, diazinon, malathion, Orthene, and car-

baryl (Sevin). Regular cleaning with vinegar and citrus (d-limonene) helps greatly, and cinnamon works as a mild repellent. If you see any scorpions, stomp them (with your shoes on) or vacuum them. Vacuuming works well for all interior bug pests, especially if a little natural diatomaceous earth (about ¼ cup) is sucked up first. That assures they go in but don't crawl out. Dust the perimeter of buildings with natural diatomaceous earth, spray citrus-based products as needed, and put out tent-shaped glue traps. Scorpions seem to love these things.

SLUGS, SNAILS, AND PILLBUGS

Under the plants, dust finely ground cedar flakes, natural diatomaceous earth, and hot pepper. Release beneficial nematodes and spray Garrett Juice plus garlic tea or citrus oil.

SOLDIER FLIES

Q. I have just discovered some brown worms in my compost. Each is about 1 inch long. Are they okay?

A. Those little beasts are probably the larvae of the black soldier flies. They are beneficial by helping to stimulate microbial activity and break down organic matter. The adult is a pretty blue-black fly that looks like a wasp. There are good photos in the *Texas Bug Book* if you want to make sure. These insects are most often present when the compost is on the moist side.

SPIDER MITES

Q. Since I moved back to Texas and started a garden, I have been plagued by red spider mites. They destroy my tomatoes, zucchini, and cucumbers. My herbs, peppers, mustard, and collards are the only plants left standing by July. Last year I went totally organic. I tried all your recipes for pest control to no avail. The neem oil didn't even work. I fear the mites will return. Three years ago when I bought the place, the soil was pretty bad, black clay and

hard packed. I brought it back to life in time with compost, lava, greensand, and other organic material. Last year the mites were worse than ever, but I had a good crop of peppers and anything they did not like, so I figure I must be doing something right. Is there anything else I can do? I'm stumped.

A. You'll be okay—you just picked the worst summer in years to make the transition to organics. When plants have spider mite infestations, it is a clear indication that they are in stress. Last summer had about sixty days of 100-degree weather and very little rain. Spider mites are telling you something even more specific. These little sap-sucking arachnids—they are not insects—attack plants that are having trouble pulling up water. Soil that's too wet or too dry can be the problem. Other reasons could include too much sun, too much shade, too much fertilizer, or too many pesticides. The solution to spider mite troubles is to plant adapted plants in healthy soil and be totally organic. You will probably see much less pest infestation this season, but if the mites do pop up, spray with any organic mix that contains seaweed. Seaweed by itself at about 2 ounces per gallon of water does a great job of ridding plants of spider mites. Dr. T. L. Senn discovered that fact years ago in research at Clemson University. Add the compost tea, natural vinegar, and molasses for even better results.

SQUASH BUGS

To control squash bugs, stink bugs, and other hard-to-kill pests, apply Tree Trunk Goop to the soil around each plant after treating the soil with beneficial nematodes. The goop functions in this case as a mulch and a very slow-release organic fertilizer. Spray the plants and soil with Garrett Juice plus garlic and citrus oil.

TARANTULAS

Q. How can I get rid of giant tarantulas?
A. The tarantulas are not only not poisonous, they are friendly and beneficial. Do not hurt them.

TERMITES

Lately there has been a rash of bad advice about termites and roots of plants hurting residential structures. For some reason, home inspectors and structural engineers have increased their warnings about having plants and mulch close to foundations. Their recommendations are to remove all natural mulch from around the house and to move large shrubs and trees away from the foundation. Some are saying not to allow trees or large shrubs to be any closer than 15 feet, or farther, from the house. Not only are these people saying not to plant, they are recommending removal of existing plants. This is extremely bad advice. Planting shrubs and trees near the foundation has been done for hundreds of years. If kept watered reasonably, plants are not a risk to properly built foundations. Nor is mulch. Tree trimmings or any other natural mulches do not encourage termites to eat your house. Termites exist on every site in every town— unless you pour enough toxic chemicals on the soil weekly to make your site glow in the dark. In an organic program, the beneficial insects and microbes will control the termites to a great degree, and organic pest control products will do the rest. Besides, having some termites on the site is beneficial. They help break down organic matter.

Q. Are there any pest control systems for a production home builder who is environmentally friendly? I am looking for a safe alternative for pest control to offer our home buyers, possibly as a standard feature, depending on cost.

A. Yes—treat the bare structural wood before covering with Bora-Care or other boric acid products, put natural DE and boric acid in the wall cavities, and use 00 sandblasting sand as a barrier around and under slabs, beams, and piers and in the plumbing leave outs. Look at the book *Common-Sense Pest Control* by Olkowski, Daar, and Olkowski for more details. Toxic chemical poisons are not necessary. This approach will be a great sales tool for your business.

Q. I am going to have some foundation work done soon, and the area of the house they are going to dig up is the same area

where I had termites a few years ago. Is there something organic I can put in the holes, before they backfill them, to discourage any more termite activity?

A. If it were my project, I'd treat the backfill soil with beneficial nematodes and then pile 00 sandblasting sand against the edge of the slab or, better still, on both sides of the beam and around the piers. This sand, also sold as 16-grit sand, creates a physical barrier for the pests. I would not use any toxic chemicals.

Q. Please advise me of what I should do to protect the house I'm building from all types of bugs. They will be sheet-rocking soon. And what should I do before they lay my sod? It is a new home for us, and we would like to keep it toxin free.

A. Dust a mix of 90 percent natural diatomaceous earth and 10 percent boric acid into the wall cavities before closing them in. You can also spray the studs, sills, and wall plates (all the raw lumber) with hot pepper spray or one of the boric acid sprays. This technique sets up a permanent pest control.

Before the sod is laid, loosen and smooth the soil, apply lava sand at 80 pounds per 1,000 square feet, cornmeal at 20 pounds per 1,000 square feet, and Texas greensand at 20 pounds per 1,000 square feet. After the sod is laid, fill in the cracks with fine-textured compost and then start the Basic Organic Program.

Q. On the side and back of my house we have a lovely herb and tomato garden, and unfortunately, we have found some termite tunnels. Pest control companies have told us that there is no organic method to get rid of termites. They will use chemicals and tell us that edible plants should not be planted in the area for a year, and it's best if nothing is planted and eaten from that area for five years! Please give me your opinion and any advice.

A. I totally agree that the toxic chemicals contaminate the soil and the plants grown in the area. I disagree that termites can't be controlled with organic and biological techniques. Acceptable tools indoors include citrus and d-limonene products, boric acid products, and EPA-registered biological products such as Bio-Blast. Tools for outside use include citrus products again, natural pyrethrum products, barriers like 00 sandblasting sand, and beneficial nematodes. The best long-term control comes from eliminating site drainage problems, as well as leaks and wet wood in the house.

THRIPS

Q. I am trying very hard to become 100 percent organic in my gardening (you should see my three-tier compost bin). However, I am having a difficult time killing the thrips that visit us every year and wreak havoc on several varieties of our flowers and many of our shrubs. Also, we have a crepe myrtle that has been languishing for some time, not growing very fast and never flowering.

A. Spray the foliage with neem now and drench the same mixture into the soil. Next year apply beneficial nematodes to the soil in early spring before bud break. Treat the root zone of the crape myrtle with horticultural cornmeal and compost. The Sick Tree Treatment is something else you should consider for the problem parts of the garden.

TICKS

Q. I called our local Extension Office to ask how to treat my yard for ticks and fleas, and they suggested I contact you. I do not want to kill the good bugs with the bad. I feed the birds and have a pet rabbit and two cats in the yard. I have not seen any fleas, but have removed several ticks from the rabbit. Can you recommend a way to kill the ticks without harming the rabbit and birds?

A. Try the following: Broadcast fine-textured cedar over the entire site. It's sold under such names as Cedar Flakes and Horticultural Cedar. Spray one of the citrus-based products such as Garden-Ville Auntie Fuego and apply beneficial nematodes. If someone tells you to use a toxic chemical such as Sevin, tell them to go jump in the lake.

TOMATO BLIGHT

Q. How do we avoid or deter the onset of yellowing leaves and the normal blight in homegrown tomato plants? I am now totally organic and growing tomatoes in that medium for the first time. I have prepared the bed with natural mulch, composted manure, greensand, lava sand, and cornmeal. What else do I need to add or do to avoid the onset of tomato wilt that has been so often my experience during my pre-organic life?

A. You are probably referring to early blight or southern blight. Any of the fungal diseases that attack tomatoes and turn the lower leaves yellow or quickly wilt the entire plant can be controlled with a combination of soil treatment and foliar spraying. Cornmeal is the key to the soil treatment. If you've already applied it, fine. If not, apply food cornmeal or, better still, horticultural cornmeal to the soil at planting at the rate of 2 pounds per 100 square feet at least. Cornmeal fights fungal diseases by stimulating beneficial microorganisms such as *Trichoderma* that eat the pathogens. It sounds as if you used the other basic ingredients. The mulch that is best for helping avoid diseases is shredded native cedar. The second step is to spray the plants at least every two weeks with Garrett Juice plus garlic tea. Neem is also effective against diseases and best used as a drench on the soil. Potassium bicarbonate can be added to the spray for added power. You should be ready for a productive year.

WASPS

Q. We are having a terrible time with wasps. My daughter is allergic to their sting.

A. Even though wasps are highly beneficial caterpillar-eating insects, I understand your need to control them. First of all, understand that they are not aggressive unless they are threatened. Some wasps, like the large cicada killers and mud daubers, would never sting unless you grabbed one— so don't do that. Other insects look like wasps but are actually flies such as hover flies, black soldier flies, and other highly beneficial insects. The already mentioned *Texas Bug Book* will help you identify these various garden critters. To repel the stinging insects, make sure, first, that you and the kids aren't wearing any scents that are attractants. In this category are not only perfumes, but also hand and body lotions, hair-sprays, makeup, and even scented soaps and deodorants. You don't have to stop using these products, just start using the unscented versions. People highly allergic to insect stings should also avoid wearing brightly colored clothing. Don't leave soda or juice containers exposed; wasps like the sweet residue. If the insects are still a problem, spray one or more of the natural repellents such as citronella, garlic-pepper tea, or orange oil sprays. Commercial products are available, or homemade brews can be made from my formulas in the free handouts.

Q. We have heard that if you paint the ceiling of a porch or patio a sky blue color that dirt daubers and wasps will not build nests there, as the color tricks them into thinking the ceiling is sky. My husband wants to use this color on the ceiling of our porch and patio. If it works, I'm willing to do it and use my utmost creative efforts to make it fit into our color scheme (which is not even close to sky blue), but if there is no fact to this at all, I don't want a sky blue porch and patio.

A. I have heard that it does actually work, but I don't know how you determine the exact shade of sky blue—morning, afternoon, hazy, ozone polluted, or what? On the other hand, I encourage the wasps. They are very beneficial because they control many species of harmful pests such as green worms, loopers, and other caterpillars. Unless someone in your family is highly allergic to stings, let the wasps hang around. They are not aggressive unless threatened. The citrus and citronella products can be used to repel them if need be.

Q. I have so many wasps and yellow jackets around my hummingbird feeders that the hummingbirds cannot eat. Any suggestions on how to keep them away?

A. The feeders that have tubes that hang down are the problem. The fluid is exposed at the tips and easily accessible to the wasps. Use the feeders that are vessels with access openings in the top. The hummingbirds can reach the sweet drink with their long beaks, but the wasps can't and will have to go elsewhere.

WEBWORMS

Q. Help! I am looking for an organic treatment for sod webworms. I know they are rare in the Dallas area, but samples have been confirmed by knowledgeable people. I just had my lawn sodded with Bermuda, and these little caterpillar-like worms come out at night and eat my grass as well as come into the house and burrow into the carpet. The people who laid the sod wanted to spray diazinon on the yard, but we didn't want to use a chemical.

A. Any of the orange-oil-based products will control them indoors as well as in the lawn. Any of the Bt (*Bacillus thuringiensis*) products will also work. Anyone who still recommends diazinon or any other neurotoxin is very foolish. They are looking for lawsuits, and the poisons simply aren't necessary. Releasing trichogramma wasps earlier in July next year will usually control the infestations.

WHITEFLIES

Q. Can whiteflies be controlled with organic techniques?

A. Yes, of course. Spray a mix of liquid seaweed and garlic-pepper tea or Garrett Juice plus garlic. Orange oil can be added at 2 ounces per gallon as a last resort. Some people use yellow sticky traps, but they are more of a monitoring device than a control, although they do help.

Pest Control Products

BAKING SODA

This natural material can be used indoors to kill ants and on all plants to help control diseases, especially those that are fungal. Sodium bicarbonate, the chemical name, is mixed at the rate of 4 teaspoons or 1 rounded tablespoon per gallon of water. It makes an excellent liquid fungicide for black spot, powdery mildew, brown patch, and other fungal problems. Potassium bicarbonate is also effective and even better for the soil. EPA-registered products are available as well as generic materials. For outdoor pest control, mix with Garrett Juice or other organic sprays.

CINNAMON

Ground cinnamon powder is very effective against ants, roaches, and other pests. It is best used indoors, but works in the garden as well. It has been reported to effectively control fire ants. This is a very powerful natural pesticide. Cinnamon oil, if you can find any, will even function as a natural herbicide. It is very powerful, so be careful.

One listener reports that cinnamon works on the little sugar ants at her house, but not on some larger ones that come in occasionally. She has sprinkled it right on them, but it didn't bother them a bit.

CITRUS OIL

Orange oil, or d-limonene, the extract from orange oil, is an important tool for organic gardeners. When added to sprays or soil drenches at very low levels (1 teaspoon to 1 ounce per gallon of water), it will help stimulate soil microbes and plant growth. At 2 ounces per gallon in a spray it will kill pest insects; at heavier rates it will even burn or kill plants. Ground citrus pulp, especially grapefruit and orange, will repel root knot nematodes and kill fire ants. Concentrated citrus oil is a solvent and will even melt plastic.

Q. I just got orange oil, but was not sure of the mixture to use or how often to spray for mosquitoes. Also, does this work for flea control on dogs? Also, how can I get rid of giant tarantulas?

A. Use any citrus concentrate at 2 ounces per gallon of water and knock those mosquitoes out of the sky whenever they are a problem. Yes, it's good for fleas and ticks on dogs when sprayed on the site or added to the bath water, but beneficial nematodes are the best site treatment for flea control. Remember that orange oil and d-limonene products are solvents. Use very small amounts in water to use on an animal's skin. Cats are very sensitive. The tarantulas are not only not poisonous, they are friendly and beneficial. Do not hurt them.

CITRUS PEELINGS

Q. Please furnish some detailed information on how to use ground-up citrus rinds for control of nematodes in a vegetable garden, around tomatoes and okra plants, etc. I have been using elbon rye for three years with no success.

A. The easiest way to use the citrus rinds, after storing them frozen, is to grind them with a blender or food processor and work the pulp into the soil prior to planting crops that are susceptible to root knot nematodes. Plants in this category include tomatoes, peppers, okra, eggplants, squash, and other row crops. Not only is the elbon rye treatment less effective, this cereal rye can become a nuisance weed in the garden.

Q. We accumulate huge quantities of citrus peels, which I freeze. I have ground up some and sprinkled them on fire ant mounds, which seems to help. The ants take it away. What other ways could I use them, and how much is okay to put in the compost pile? Since the citrus kills beneficials, I am afraid it will kill the microbes in the compost, too. Also, how much fireplace ash is safe to compost? I read your recent article on not composting grill ashes, but it wasn't clear how much fireplace ash was okay.

A. The citrus won't hurt the microbes or beneficial insects unless you spray the concentrated oil mixes. It sounds as if you are doing well. Fireplace ashes can be used to make up about 10–20 percent of the compost pile, but a smaller percentage would be better.

CORN GLUTEN MEAL

In the early 1990s, Dr. Nick Christians and his research students at Iowa State discovered that corn gluten meal, a product of the wet milling process, works as a pre-emergent weed and feed. It inhibits weed root formation during germination. With a nitrogen content of about 10 percent, it is also a powerful fertilizer.

Apply at about 20 pounds per 1,000 square feet—just like a fertilizer application. In North Texas, do it about March 1 and again about June 1 for even greater control. Unlike chemical herbicides, corn gluten meal replaces the need to buy additional fertilizer.

Warning: Do not allow a bag of corn gluten meal to get wet. The resultant odor is overwhelming, and pets can get sick if they eat it.

I can tell by the overload of questions that there is still much confusion about cornmeal and corn gluten meal. They are very different products and have greatly different horticultural uses. Cornmeal is a fungal disease fighter and algae control. It is broadcast at 15–20 pounds to control fungal diseases and at 150 pounds per surface acre of water to control algae.

You can use about one-half pound per 100 square feet in your back-yard fish pond. You can use it any day year-round.

Cornmeal has no power to directly control weeds. That's where corn gluten meal (CGM) comes in. CGM is the protein portion of cornmeal, making up less than 10 percent of the complete product. Corn gluten meal is a natural weed-and-feed fertilizer. CGM is broadcast in the spring around March 1 to prevent grassburs, crabgrass, and other annual weeds that germinate from seed in the spring. For the cool-season weeds, broadcast sometime around October 1 at 15–20 pounds per 1,000 square feet for the control of henbit, dandelions, annual bluegrass, and other winter weeds. It also serves as a powerful organic fertilizer having about 10 percent nitrogen.

CGM can be used when overseeding with ryegrass or other cool-season crops, but only with care. You must wait until the grass, vetch, or clover has germinated and started to grow before putting the corn gluten meal down or the seed germination will be hurt. On the other hand, if all you want is organic fertilizer, it may not be the best choice. Corn gluten meal is more expensive than other organic fertilizers that work as well or better in that regard.

On another issue, corn gluten meal continues to be available in powder form and in granulated form. Which is best is still a debate. The CGM powder probably gives more thorough weed control, but the granulated form is far less dusty and messy. Try them both and see which works best for you.

Cornmeal has no substantial herbicidal qualities, and corn gluten meal has no substantial disease-fighting qualities.

Q. I spend fifteen dollars for a bag of corn gluten, three dollars for pendamethilin. The pendamethilin leaves me with acute toxicity every time I use it. Symptoms: dilated pupils, extreme dehydration, "drugged feeling," and loss of appetite. The EPA has said this product is nontoxic! I can't afford to pay for the overpriced bag of corn by-product. Please help. I am beginning to glow in the dark. I am also a student of horticulture aspiring to become a landscape architect. Any comments?

A. What's your health worth? Also, the corn gluten meal serves as your first round of organic fertilizer, and fewer annual applications are needed. The organic approach is easier, works better, costs less, and is much better for your health. I don't understand the problem. There's an even cheaper way to manage the weeds— mow 'em.

Q. Will corn gluten meal kill native buffalograss? Is now the time to put down corn gluten meal in the Texas Panhandle? It will freeze very soon.

A. It will not hurt any existing grass. It only prevents the growth of seedlings as they first emerge. After plants are growing, corn gluten meal serves as an excellent organic fertilizer. The timing for application is just before the seeds start to germinate.

CORNMEAL

Cornmeal works as a natural disease fighter in the soil. It stimulates beneficial microorganisms (*Trichoderma* and others) that feed on pest microbes such as *Rhizoctonia*—better known as brown patch in St. Augustine.

Cornmeal applied at about 2 pounds per 100 square feet also helps to prevent damping-off and any other soilborne fungal diseases on food and ornamental crops. One application may be all that is needed if you are on the organic program.

Cornmeal needs moisture to activate. Multiple applications are okay if needed because cornmeal serves as a mild organic fertilizer. Rain won't hurt its efficacy because, like most organic products, it is not water soluble.

Natural cornmeal is the very best fungal disease control available. It can be used for rose problems, photinia problems, damping-off in your seedlings, and for brown patch in St. Augustinegrass. It works in potting plants as well. Use at about 2 pounds per 100 square feet. In pots, use 1 heaping tablespoon per gallon of soil. Corn gluten meal, the protein fraction of cornmeal is a powerful natural weed-and-feed fertilizer. Apply it at 20 pounds per 1,000 square feet in the early spring and early fall. Water it in immediately after application and then allow the area to dry out for a while.

Q. I have already put down some cornmeal to fight the brown patch problem in my yard. The night after I put it down we had heavy rains. Should I put more down? I also need help treating my rosemary. It is well established, but the leaves look spotty. The spots are light green in color, and when I shake the plant, small winged bugs fly out. How do I get rid of the culprits and still be able to use the herb for consumption?

A. Rain won't hurt the cornmeal at all; it probably helps to activate it. Cornmeal might also be the answer to the rosemary problem. Rosemary is a wonderful culinary herb and landscape perennial. Not only is the foliage excellent for cooking and herb teas, the flower stems are great for cutting, and they can be used for garnish and table decoration. Plus, the beautiful light blue flowers are edible. The plant does have one fault, and you are probably experiencing it. Because of its incredibly dense and fibrous root system, the plant's watering needs to be done carefully. Rosemary is one of those plants that can easily be overwatered and severely stressed, but it is also fairly easily underwatered, causing the plant to dry out and go into stress. Sounds like you may be new to the natural approach, so add the rock powders, lava sand or Volcanite, also compost and cornmeal. Make sure the beds drain well, but don't let them dry out.

Q. Your note on the effectiveness of cornmeal in controlling soilborne fungi makes me wonder about its ability to control cotton root rot in grapes. Has anyone tested this? How should it be applied? Should I work it into the soil?

A. It appears to work on all species of pathogenic fungi. Apply it to the soil at 10–20 pounds per 1,000 square feet and gently work into the soil. The shredded native cedar as a mulch will also help. I assume you are already using an organic program and doing regular foliar feeding.

Cornmeal works as a disease fighter in the soil by providing and stimulating existing beneficial microorganisms that feed on pathogens such as *Rhizoctonia,* better known as brown patch in St. Augustine. Cornmeal at about two pounds per 100 square feet also helps seedlings avoid damping-off disease.

Cornmeal's most interesting and popular use came to us from

one of my listeners. It appears to be a cure for toe and fingernail fungus, ringworm, athlete's foot, jock itch, and even psoriasis and other skin problems. Ranchers have used cornmeal to treat ringworm, udder warts, ear fungus, and other problems. See my web site, www.dirtdoctor.com, for more information.

DIATOMACEOUS EARTH

Natural diatomaceous earth is the skeletal remains of fresh- or saltwater diatoms. It consists of mostly silica but also contains aluminum, sodium, iron, and lots of trace minerals, including some that are rare.

Natural diatomaceous earth is dug from the earth, ground into a powder, and sold as an anticaking agent for stored foods and grains, a natural insecticide, and a natural food supplement for pets and livestock. It is approved by the USDA for use in food at up to 2 percent of the food volume.

Natural diatomaceous earth should be added to the food of all pets and livestock. At present, Muenster Natural dog and cat foods are the only products on the market that contain the proper levels of diatomaceous earth (DE). Some animals, like sheep and cattle, will eat it by free choice. Horses and most pets need to have it mixed into their food.

Swimming-pool-filter DE has been calcined—partially melted—and often chemically treated. It is dangerous to breathe because of the high level of crystalline silica. It has no use other than in swimming-pool filters.

Swimming-pool DE and DE treated with other chemicals are totally unacceptable for any horticulture or animal use. The diatomaceous earth that is acceptable for pest control in an organic program and for use as a feed supplement for animals is a totally natural material dug out of the ground and put in a bag. It has not been heated and partially melted, as has swimming-pool DE, and it has had no other ingredients added. Natural and feed-grade DE are basically the same. Some DE products, for example, contain pyrethrum and PBO, which is piperonyl butoxide. Pyrethrum is a very powerful natural insecticide. PBO is a synthetic chemical synergist that can negatively affect the liver. People should use only natural DE for all gardening and pet uses.

Q. I have some food-grade diatomaceous earth and want to know how to use it for a bad flea infestation and for plant pests. Can I put it on the dogs with a shaker, like a salt shaker?

A. Yes, just don't apply more than once every two weeks. It is drying on their skin. It's perfectly safe for the dogs for topical use and as a food additive. In fact, I recommend putting it in their feed daily at 2 percent of the volume.

Q. Can I use it in the house on the carpet?

A. Yes, just don't overdo and be sure to vacuum the excess.

Q. I thought about mixing it with water and spraying it in a pressure sprayer. Will that work?

A. Yes, after the DE dries, it will have the desiccating and insect-killing qualities. It will also kill beneficial insects, so the method should only be used on pest-infested plants. It won't work to control fleas on the site, only on the animals. The reason? There are no adult fleas on the site, just eggs, larvae, and pupae. The adults are only on the animals.

Q. For outside, I thought about mixing it with a fertilizer so I could broadcast it. Will that work?

A. Mixing DE with fertilizer is a good way to treat crickets, chinch bugs, and other pests, and give the soil a good trace mineral treatment.

Q. Do you have a better solution to the flea problem?

A. Yes, bathing the dogs with mild herbal shampoos and applying beneficial nematodes are by far the best treatments for not only fleas and ticks but also grubs, termites, roaches, chinch bugs, fire ants, termites, thrips, and other pest insects that have soil-dwelling life cycles.

D-LIMONENE—SEE ORANGE OIL

DORMANT OIL

Q. What are the temperature and weather restrictions on using dormant oil for control of insect pests?

A. Dormant (horticultural) oil should be used when there is no rain in the forecast and the temperature is between 40 and 80 degrees. As with all sprays, while using it be sure to keep the spray shaken well or plant damage can result. However, don't use it at all if you have healthy populations of beneficial insects—it will kill them too.

GARLIC

The juice of garlic cloves is an effective insect and disease control. Its use should be limited, however, to avoid repelling beneficial insects. Garlic is systemic in plants, just as it is in the human body and therefore effective as a preventative on pest-prone plants. It is a very important part of my organic rose program and the organic pecan and fruit tree program. Garlic tea can be made per my homemade formula or bought commercially.

HYDROGEN PEROXIDE

Hydrogen peroxide (H_2O_2) is the equivalent of a water molecule with an extra oxygen atom. It can be used as a disinfectant, an antiseptic, and a bleach.

It comes in concentrations from 3 to 100 percent. The 100 percent variety is used in rocket fuel. All our purposes can be served with the 3 percent version that's available at grocery stores and pharmacies.

This colorless, odorless liquid is not a stable compound. It must be protected from light and kept in a cool place.

Hydrogen peroxide can be poured on minor cuts and scrapes. It will foam as it breaks down to water and the extra oxygen—a gas that bubbles to the surface. The high concentration of oxygen kills bacteria. The same is true with plants. I recommend splashing it on wounds on trees.

LAVA SAND

This sand-sized and smaller waste material left from lava

gravel is an excellent, high-energy soil-amendment material. Finer-textured material is even better. It can be used in potting soils, germination media, and bed preparation. Lava sand, or lava in any size, increases the water-holding capacity of the soil and increases the paramagnetism. The result is increased production of any plant crop. Broadcast at 40–80 pounds per 1,000 square feet, 1 ton per acre, or till into new beds at 80–150 pounds per 1,000 square feet. If possible, use lava sands with high paramagnetic count. Lava sand offers a physical improvement to the soil that moves unhealthy, unbalanced soils toward balance. The mineral makeup of lava sand is less important than the shape of each piece of sand. The angular, porous pieces of lava hold and exchange nutrients efficiently, and they attract and redistribute cosmic energy in the soil. Cosmic energy is a fancy term for the sun's energy.

Lava sand is magical stuff. Dr. Phil Callahan, the scientist who probably understands more about the secrets of nature than anyone on earth, taught me to teach people to add lava sand to the soil. When he explains why, it sounds so simple and makes so much sense, but when I try to explain it, there's often something lost in the translation. Here are some of the ways to use lava sand for greater plant production. **Bed preparation**—till together with compost and organic fertilizer. Use 40–80 pounds per 1,000 square feet. **Potting soil**—add up to one-third the volume of good potting soil. **Roses**—add to rose bed preparation at 80 pounds per 1,000 square feet and to the top of roses in pots at a rate heavy enough to cover the soil surface red. Gently work into the top 1 inch. **Sick trees**—broadcast under the trees at 40–80 pounds per 1,000 square feet. For more effective results on sicker trees, drill 2-inch holes 12–18 inches deep throughout the root zone and fill with 50 percent lava sand, 25 percent compost, and 25 percent cornmeal. **Turf**—broadcast at 40 pounds per 1,000 square feet.

Lava sand—magic? No, it just helps the physics, chemistry, and biology of the soil. Shortly after I had turned North Texas and Oklahoma on to this fascinating natural material, the questions started coming in. "Okay, it's working great, but why? What's in lava sand that's making plants respond so strongly?"

At this point, I really didn't know for sure other than what Dr. Callahan had told me about energy and paramagnetism. I knew that trying to explain paramagnetic energy to organic gardeners would be difficult, and explaining it to organiphobes would be a total waste of time. So, I tried another angle: a soil test. I sent some lava sand, which had been brought into the Dallas/Fort Worth area from New Mexico, to K. Chandler at Texas Plant and Soil Labs in Edinburgh. The results were interesting but puzzling. The nutrient value was almost nil and the pH was 8.2. How was this stuff working to make plants grow so well? I had never seen any chlorosis (iron deficiency) come on from using lava around susceptible plants such as sweetgum, dogwood, or photinia. In fact, I saw just the opposite. Yellowing plants greened up. How could that be? It could be because pH is an indicator only—not a controller. Many factors in the soil are more important than pH. Lava sand addresses those factors. Lava has an unusual exchange capacity, meaning that it has the ability to hold and make available lots of mineral nutrients. Lava also holds water, just at the right level for a long time. If the soil has good moisture, microbes and earthworms will be benefited.

MOLASSES

Sweet syrup that is a carbohydrate used as a soil amendment to feed and stimulate microorganisms. Contains sulfur, potash, and many trace minerals. Approximate analysis is 1-0-5. Molasses is a good, quick source of energy for the soil life and microbes in a compost pile, and it will chase fire ants away. It is a carbon source and feeds beneficial microbes, creating greater nature fertility. Liquid molasses is used in sprays, and dry molasses is used as an ingredient in organic fertilizers. Excellent foliar-feeding material and can be mixed with other organic liquids. Use at 2–4 quarts per acre for soil application. For foliar application on broadleaf plants, use 1 pint per acre. For grasses and grains, still use 1 quart per acre. Blackstrap molasses, which is hard to find, is the best choice because it contains the sulfur and iron of the original material, but any kind will work. Molasses is the best sugar for horticultural use because of its trace minerals.

Dry molasses isn't really straight dried molasses. It's molasses sprayed on a grain residue carrier.

NOSEMA

Nosema locustae is a biological control for crickets and grasshoppers. It works the same way Bt works on caterpillars. It's applied as a dry bait, the insects eat the material, get sick, and are cannibalized by their friends. Charming, isn't it? But it works. Brand names include Nolo Bait, Grasshopper Attack, and Semispore. It is very effective on the young grasshoppers or nymphs but has questionable effectiveness on adult grasshoppers.

ORANGE OIL (D-LIMONENE)

The concentrated oil from citrus fruit. D-limonene is the commercial extracted product that is used for cleaning and insect control.

D-limonene is the major component of the oil extracted from citrus rind. It has always been used for its fragrance and flavoring qualities, but in the past decade it has been one of the fastest-growing segments of the household-cleaning market.

Orange oil is available commercially, or you can make your own. Put a bunch of citrus peelings in a container and cover them with water. Let them sit for a couple of days, then strain off the liquid. You can extract more oil by simmering the peelings.

The strength of homemade orange oil varies significantly, so you'll have to experiment when using it in the recipes that follow. It's impossible to duplicate the concentration of commercial orange oil or d-limonene.

Orange oil is a pleasant-smelling solvent. Commercial d-limonene at full strength can replace a wide variety of products, including mineral spirits, methyl ethyl ketone, acetone, toluene, and glycol ethers. So be careful when using strong solutions, since it can melt plastic and ruin paint finishes. For most of our purposes, 1–2 ounces per gallon of water should be the maximum concentration.

PEPPER

Commercial hot pepper products are available, but homemade powders are easy. Just dry the peppers, grind, and store dry. Some liquid commercial pepper products have wax that helps keep the spray on plant leaves. Garlic-pepper tea is even more effective, but it is not yet available commercially. Hot pepper can be used to repel insects and large furry animal pests as well. Habanero is my favorite because it's the hottest.

TOXIC PRODUCTS

MSMA

Q. I've lived here twelve years and have enjoyed the wildflowers, ladybugs, and caterpillars that come around every spring. However, this spring I have seen (and smelled) the city spraying some chemical over the area. We have no flowers or insects, only ugly brown dirt. My kids see lots of tadpole eggs in the water, but never any tadpoles. This water runs into a small pond at the end of my street. The city said they are spraying two chemicals—Trimec and MSMA. The guy gave me the usual spiel. It won't hurt the environment if "used correctly" and it won't run off into the water. He said it causes no health problems and is perfectly safe (yeah, right). He said there is a city ordinance that says grass cannot get over 12 inches high, and they are trying to grow Bermudagrass instead of the weeds.

A. Your note is very frustrating. Trimec contains three toxic synthetic herbicides, and the "A" in MSMA stands for arsenic. These toxic pesticides kill not only the targeted weeds but also other plants that are important for our biodiversity. The arsenic compound in MSMA (also DSMA) delivers a basic element that is not only famous for killing people, it is accumulative and continues to build up in the environment and in your pets and in you and your family. Maybe contacting the city council members would help, but it's very difficult to get an organic message through sometimes, since these toxic products are so widely recommended, sold, and used. The ironic point is that the mix of various grasses and wildflowers is prettier and much easier to maintain than a mono-culture of Bermudagrass. The large noxious weeds can be killed with vinegar sprays, and the best way to control the general height is by mowing. More and more cities are starting to employ ranch-ers with goat herds. This low-tech approach is effective and inter-esting, especially for the kids—both kinds.

Weed-and-Feed Fertilizers

As of this writing, many of the heavily recommended "weed-and-feed" fertilizers still contain Atrazine, which is a toxic chemical herbicide that is quite effective in killing your trees and shrubs. One of the most interesting points about these products is that nonorganic people agree with me that these products should not be used. Although the "chemicals are okay" crowd have no problem with synthetic fertilizers and herbicides, they do acknowledge that the two ingredients aren't suitable to be applied at the same time. The pre-emergent her-bicide part of the products needs to be applied about two months earlier than the soluble fertilizer part of the product. Plus, we agree that Atrazine should not be used on residential property because the roots of trees cover the entire property of most lots. Some of the specific products that you should avoid are Scotts Bonus S, Vigoro, Sam's, and other similar products. The other point is that April is too late to use any pre-emergent, including the natural choice, corn gluten meal. Corn gluten meal can still be used as a powerful organic fertilizer, but the herbicide window has passed.

VINEGAR

Q. What do you mean by "natural apple cider vinegar"? Given the "natural" qualifier at the beginning of the phrase, does that

mean it's not the apple cider vinegar I buy at my local grocery store?

A. Apple cider vinegar is usually the natural stuff. The label will say that it is 5 percent or 50 grain. This product is actually made from apples. Avoid products that use the term "apple cider *flavored.*" These products are human-made white vinegar or acetic acid with color added. Vinegar is one of my critics' favorite subjects. Their common argument is that there is no difference in the two products, that they are both merely acetic acid and contain no trace minerals. Only problem for them is that I have these pesky tests that show that the natural vinegars have considerably more minerals, especially potassium, calcium, phosphorous, and iron. That's why natural vinegar works so well as a horticultural tool.

The natural vinegars, which can also be made from other fruit and sugar sources, are the choice for fertilizers and sprays. Use the natural vinegars at 1 tablespoon per gallon of irrigation water for all potted plants and at about 1 ounce per gallon in foliar sprays. Apple cider vinegar is one of the ingredients in the Garrett Juice formula. It's also good with oil on your salad. The white distilled vinegars are the choice when killing something is the plan. Pickling vinegar (10 percent or 100 grain) sprayed full strength with 2 ounces of orange oil or d-limonene and 1 tablespoon of liquid soap will kill most weeds. It will also burn or kill your good plants, so be careful. Products of 20 percent vinegar are now available in organic gardening stores and feed stores. It will kill weeds by itself. There are also commercial organic herbicides available now that contain vinegar as the active ingredient. Avoid those that contain glacial acetic acid, which is a petroleum derivative.

Landscaping and Garden Maintenance

Landscaping is the subject with which I have the greatest comfort. The most curious fact about this subject is that landscaping plants are by far the easiest to grow organically—food crops are much more difficult—yet landscaping people have put up the most resistance. It's very easy. Hopefully this will help.

AZALEAS

Azaleas need a totally artificial bed built with 100 percent organic matter. The Azalea Society recommends 50 percent peat moss and 50 percent fine-textured pine bark mix with synthetic fertilizers added. What I have found to work better and last much longer is 50 percent well-finished compost and 50 percent fine-textured horticultural cedar. Per cubic yard of mix, add 5 gallons of lava sand, 1 gallon of Texas greensand, and 1 gallon of cornmeal. If you add a little more compost/lava sand mix (about 1 inch) and about 2–3 inches of shredded native cedar mulch every year, you will probably never have to tear out and rebuild the beds, as the other technique requires. Be sure to moisten the mixture thoroughly before it is placed in the bed.

Azaleas should be pruned, if needed, right after the spring bloom to help maintain a compact form. Pick-pruning is best, but a light shearing is acceptable too. Pruning in the winter will ruin the spring blooms.

BULBS

Q. Last year I planted some spring bulbs and want to plant many more this year. I have been told to refrigerate them for several weeks before planting. I do not have much room in the refrigerator. Can they be put in a freezer, or is that too cold?

A. Some bulbs need cold hours and some don't. Grape hyacinths, narcissus, and daffodils need no cold treatment and should be planted in the fall. On the other hand, Dutch hyacinths and tulips do need about six weeks of chilling at 40–45 degrees prior to planting in mid to late December. The problem is that most refrigerators are kept at about 35 degrees. The freezer would be far too cold. Some good garden centers will keep the bulbs in storage for you at the right temperature. Be sure to make the beds fluffy by preparing them with compost, lava sand, cornmeal, and Texas greensand. Per 100 square feet of bed area, use about 10 pounds of lava sand, 5 pounds of Texas greensand, and 2½ pounds of horticultural cornmeal. If no compost has been added to the bed in a while, apply about a 4-inch layer across the entire bed. Mix all this material together into the existing soil to create a fluffy raised bed that the bulbs will love. Plant them at a depth of about twice the length of the bulbs. For even better results, add a thin layer of shredded native cedar as a mulch at about 1–1½ inches.

BURNING LEAVES

Q. We have started the cleanup of vines and clearing of some of the heavier layers of leaves (mosquito haven). Our dilemma is a controversy over burning small piles of leaves in the treed areas. I say that we should not burn over the tree root systems because the heat from the burning leaves might hurt the roots close to the surface.

A. It's a foolish thing to do from several standpoints. The heat from the fire will injure the tree roots. Burning leaves is also a fire hazard and a source of air pollution, but there's one more problem, and it is the most significant. Leaves are a valuable source of organic matter and natural nutrients. The best leaf management is to let them stay where they fall just as the forest does. Mulching them with the lawn mower reduces the volume. The second best procedure is to put them in the compost pile, make compost, and then return the material to where it came from in the first place. Burning leaves and other organic matter from your site is the same as burning up your money. The best fertilizer is recycled dead organic matter from plants that grew on your land. The mosquitoes can be done in with a spraying of a citrus-based product.

DETOXIFYING CONTAMINATED SOIL

Q. We moved into a new house late this summer, and on one side of the house there is a thin- to medium-depth layer of gravel, so they wouldn't have to mow that area. I want to plant in that area, and I will have some raised beds but not everywhere. Will I have to remove the gravel before I can begin any bed preparation, or can I leave it there?

A. It would probably be best to remove the gravel—for one reason, to make sure the previous owners didn't put plastic under it. When people create a gravel utility area, they often treat the soil with nasty toxic chemical herbicides. As a precaution, detoxify the area while you build the new beds. After removal of the unwanted material, drench the area with the activated-carbon product NORIT or GroSafe. Next, drench the area with Garrett Juice plus 2 ounces of orange oil or d-limonene per gallon. Then add about 4 inches compost, lava sand at 80 pounds per 1,000 square feet, 40 pounds of Texas greensand, 10 pounds of dry molasses, and 20 pounds of horticultural cornmeal. Organic fertilizer should also be added at 10 pounds. This bed preparation will be sufficient for most ornamentals, herbs, and food crops. Specialty crops like roses, gardenias, and camellias need even greater quantities of the same ingredients. Totally unadapted plants like azaleas and rhododendrons need even more.

EARTHWORM SUICIDE

Q. A large number of earthworms crawled from my yard onto the sidewalk, died, and dried up. This has been occurring over the past week and a half. We are trying to be organic and have not used any chemicals in quite a while. Any ideas as to what may have caused this? All the dead worms sort of remind me of lemmings jumping and following each other over a cliff.

A. Earthworms committing suicide happens on all sites. It's a curiosity that many people have puzzled over. The best explanation I've heard is that vibrations in the soil run the worms out. We know it's not the water, because the worms will often leave the soil, travel across paved decks, and drown themselves in pools and water features. Electrical currents in the soil have also been suggested, but the most likely culprits are gasoline or diesel engines and thunder.

EROSION

Q. We have just bought a house that backs onto a creek. The bank is very steep and goes down about 15 feet. We have removed by hand most of the poison ivy threatening to take over the back yard, and now we are looking for something to plant to prevent erosion. The area is steep and has partial sun in the mornings. Do you have recommendations? We would like something that will grow fairly quickly and needs little to no attention.

A. Several of the tough ground covers will grow in this situation. Take a look at purple wintercreeper, liriope, and even Asian jasmine. My favorite plant for this condition is inland seaoats. It is a very strong perennial native grass. It's pretty and will spread from the decorative seed heads that form in the fall. For a fast solution, cover the area with shredded tree trimmings. This material will lock in place and prevent erosion from all events except massive floods.

FALL IS FOR PLANTING

Yes, there's a lot going on in the fall—school projects, football, catching up from summer vacations, etc., but this is the best time of the year to do most major planting. No, the spring is not the best time. Other than the nurseries having a bigger stock of plants, spring is about the worst time to do landscape planting. You can get away with doing the planting then, but autumn is such a better choice. The period from late summer to fall is simply the ideal time for planting permanent plants.

When trees, shrubs, vines, ground covers, and perennials are planted in the late summer, the new plants have the advantage of the burst of root growth in the fall. Trees, shrubs, and other woody plants have a significant spurt of root growth in October, November, and often December. They also have some root growth in the winter. The result is a plant or plants that are not in stress and take off growing aggressively in the spring. Plants installed in the late summer and early fall will have far less transplant shock, will establish easier, and will start to grow at a rate that will surprise you.

There's another reason that fall is the best time for planting. The garden centers and feed stores have more time to help you and the prices are usually the best of the year. Why fight the crowds in the spring? Shop and plant in the fall.

One more point. Not every year, but most years, we have a window of great weather from late summer until the first freeze when many plants will grow well and put on quite a show. For example, this is the best time of the year to plant and enjoy marigolds, nasturtiums, mums, asters, and zinnias. Petunias, Johnny-jump-ups, pansies, dianthus, and flowering kale can also be planted now, and they will grow right into the freezing weather. Light frosts make some of the cool-season plants more compact and have better flower production. It's also a great time to plant cool-season vegetables such as lettuce, cabbage, broccoli, Brussels sprouts, Swiss chard, carrots, sugar snap beans, arugula, coriander, kohlrabi, garlic, winter squash, lima beans, cauliflower, and various greens.

FLOWER FRAGRANCE

Q. This may be a really dumb question, but is there anything in the soil or water that affects the fragrance of flowers? I have some flowering plants that are supposed to smell wonderful—an angel's trumpet that has no odor at all, a sweet autumn clematis that has very little fragrance, roses that smelled wonderful when I bought them but have less and less perfume as time goes by.

Also, you have a list of recommended plants to which you might add the shrimp plant and the lemon lollipop. I have a combination of shade and lousy to nonexistent soil. It is a standing joke in my house that stuff does not bloom for me, and existing blossoms generally fall off within forty-eight hours of going in the ground. However, I planted both the shrimp plant and lemon lollipop this spring, and they went bananas. Neither has stopped blooming since they went in the ground in April. They are wonderful, but I had never heard of either of them before.

A. Good tip. I like those plants, too. And yes, the soil can affect several plant characteristics—overall size, leaf color, flower color, fragrance, timing and length of bloom, and also taste of food crops. Location in regard to sun and shade can also affect those same characteristics. Taste and food value are controlled by how well trace minerals are getting into the plants. Using the organic fertilizers and amendments and encouraging life in the soil is the answer. Start the Basic Organic Program now if you haven't already. For a plant to keep exactly the original flower and fragrance color, the growing conditions must be the same as they were in the nursery. Of course, that isn't always possible or even desired.

FOLIAR FEEDING

Q. I spray Garrett Juice on grapes, raspberries, fruit trees, pecan trees, onions, cabbage, and flower beds. The way the weather is, I can't get more than two or three days' break between rains. When do the plants get the most benefit from the spray? Once applied, how long before all of the benefit is received and rain will not matter?

A. In general, foliar-feeding sprays are the most effective early in the morning and at dusk. When the weather is cool and moist, the pores (stomata) are open and receptive. Just before a rain is a good time to get nutrients into leaves. The nutrients enter and affect the plant almost immediately, so a rain following a spraying does not ruin the application. In fact, when the rain washes the excess residue off leaves, the soil receives a little fertilizer. Since the rain will leach a small amount of nutrients from the leaves, the ideal time to do foliar-spray feeding is immediately after a rain. If the spraying is being done for insect control, the best time to spray is at dusk or at night because the liquids will stay wet on the leaves in the dark longer. Does that cause disease problems? No, not with an organic program. The organic products stimulate beneficial microorganisms, which help to control the pathogens.

FUNGI

Q. We have some old tree roots just under the surface of the grass. There are many large fungi or molds that have come to the surface. They are hard clumps, but can be broken off by foot. What can I do to get rid of them?

A. Probably nothing to worry about. If there are other trees in the area, those growths are quite likely the fruiting bodies of beneficial organisms called mycorrhizal fungi. That indicates that the soil is in healthy condition. If there are no other trees, the growths are most likely the fruiting bodies of fungi working on breaking down the old decaying roots. In either event, nothing is needed other than to continue the Basic Organic Program. If they continue to be an unsightly problem, apply horticultural cornmeal at 15 pounds per 1,000 square feet and spray with potassium bicarbonate at 1 rounded tablespoon per gallon of water.

GARDENIAS

Gardenias are not always easy to grow, but the best results come from a comprehensive program of planting them in rich beds, fertilizing with organic fertilizers, and adding a tablespoon of vinegar per gallon of irrigation water. Bed prep for gardenias is: 4 inches compost, 1 inch wheat bran/cornmeal/molasses mix, ½ inch lava sand, ¼ inch Texas greensand, and one of the organic fertilizers at 20 pounds per square feet. Also spray the foliage every two weeks with Garrett Juice, which contains vinegar, or a fish and seaweed product. If vinegar isn't in the product you choose, add it at 1 ounce per gallon of spray. The other ingredients are also important.

GROUND-COVER CHOICES

Q. I have bare spots in my yard that are shady. The soil is compacted clay, which I am planning to aerate. I have also added red lava sand, greensand, and worm castings. What kind of grass or other cover can I plant that will grow well in shade? Also what else can I do to get the soil healthy?

A. Very common question. In shady areas where grass growing is a problem, it's best to give up the turf idea and go the ground-cover route. Choices include English ivy, ophiopogon, liriope, Asian jasmine, and our native called horseherb. Sometimes it's best to use just shredded mulch or gravel with no planting. My favorite gravel is decomposed granite. The contrast is pleasant, and the trees love this treatment. No more bed preparation is needed if you plant horseherb, but add about 2 inches of compost before planting the other choices. Since you'll be working in the roots of trees, the bed prep should be done with a turning fork and the trowel as the transplants are planted. Rototilling would destroy all the trees' feeder roots—so don't do that.

HOLLIES

Q. My husband wants to shorten some holly bushes in our front yard. They are growing up against the house and are 6 feet tall. Don't know the variety. He would like to cut them back to 2 feet. Will this hurt them, will they grow out and look pretty, when should he do it? Should I treat them with anything afterward? I am totally organic and have been for at least five years. The bushes face the south.

A. The hollies are facing disaster. Pruning that severely will damage the plants, and they may never be the same. Some hollies are tough and can grow back to look decent again, but don't be fooled that the plants will like this treatment. The better approach is to remove the shrubs and replant dwarf plants such as dwarf yaupon holly, dwarf Chinese holly, Carissa holly, or compact nandina. If the pruning is done, the best timing is late winter just before bud break. The worst time would be in the spring. The stress would be the most severe, and you'll have to look at dehorned bare stems the rest of the summer, fall, and all winter long.

HORSEHERB

Q. We have sections of our lawn that are shaded so well that we cannot keep our turf grass growing. Is there a ground cover you recommend? Some of these areas are high-traffic areas—others are not.

A. We have a native, shade-tolerant ground cover that can take traffic—horseherb (*Calyptocarpus*). It requires little water or fertilizer but does go bare in the winter. You could also use English ivy, Asian jasmine, or ophiopogon with natural stone stepping-stones for the foot traffic. Two other favorite native choices of mine are snakeroot and frog fruit.

HYACINTH BEANS

Q. I've grown hyacinth beans for the past three years, and they've always been in bloom before this time of the year. This year I have beautiful vines but not a single blossom. I harvested the seed from last year's plants for this year's vines. Do you have any idea why they might not be blooming? Is there any way to encourage them?

A. Mine are doing the same. The problem started this past winter. It was too mild, and the beans sprouted and started growing far too early. Then we had a long, cool spring. Then more problems—remember how cool the first part of the summer was? This was all very pleasant for us, but the plants were confused and started to bloom considerably earlier than normal, although it was a weak, puny bloom. When the hot weather finally came, it hit hard. The plants weren't prepared and suffered. The extreme hot and dry weather has lasted a long time. The plants simply don't like those weird conditions, especially when they all come in the same season. There may still be a second flowering and a production of seed, but we're running out of time.

Q. Is hyacinth bean pod edible?

A. Yes, but only when the bean pods are very young. They get tough quickly as they mature. I have not tried cooking the beautiful black-and-white seeds. You might ask the people at BRIT, which is Botanical Research Institute of Texas, 817-332-4441. The vine is best used as a gorgeous ornamental. Next year try big red rippers for the most delicious peas you have ever tasted.

HYACINTHS

Q. I planted hyacinth and daffodil bulbs in the fall, thinking we would have a normal year. Lo and behold, we had an extended summer, and all the bulbs are up about a foot. Is there anything I can do to save them and make them bloom in the spring, or will they bloom now and get frozen?

A. They will probably get frozen. Next year wait to plant the Dutch hyacinths and tulips until late December after the air and soil have cooled. The daffodils will probably be fine, but you might want to add some additional fluffy mulch, such as partially decomposed leaves. The hyacinths may not do very well this year. They need the cool hours, just as tulips do.

HYDROPONIC GARDENING

Q. I have developed rheumatoid arthritis, which is seriously affecting the enjoyment I have always received by gardening. I would like to start hydrogardening, since I would be able to do it without any bending and having to control the weeds. Can you help by giving the information on how to start this project? Can it be done organically? I would like to start this project in my greenhouse over the winter.

A. I know very little about hydrogardening or hydroponics, but I am not a big fan of that approach because of the lack of soil. Soil is the most important part of the natural system. I'm not sure how you can get the proper level of trace minerals and living organisms in a liquid system. If you want to try, use the liquid organic products such as fish emulsion and seaweed, liquid humate, Garrett Juice, and biostimulants such as Medina. How to get the rock minerals into the system will be the biggest challenge. I'm not sure how to liquefy lava sand and Texas greensand. You might want to consider an alternative plan—building raised beds and using soil.

INDIAN HAWTHORN

Q. I am having a problem with my four-to-five-year-old dwarf Indian hawthorn bushes. They are in a well-drained bed on the back side of my house and receive full sun all afternoon. They have shredded cypress mulch around them. I don't see any pests on the leaves or stems. The leaves first have reddish purple spots and then just turn red and eventually fall off. I have about ten of them, and all have the problem to some degree. What do I need to do?

A. This is the same disease infestation that plagues photinias. The fungal leaf spot is a secondary symptom. The real problem is in the root zone. Like photinias, Indian hawthorns have weak roots that are easily attacked by fungal diseases, especially when beds are poorly prepared, drainage is bad, or heavy chemical use is practiced. The symptoms only start to show on the foliage after the roots are in deep trouble. The solution is the Sick Tree Treatment— aeration, organic soil amendments, and foliar sprays that contain Garrett Juice and potassium bicarbonate. I don't recommend cypress mulch. Shredded native tree trimmings are cheaper, breathe better, and encourage more healthy plant growth. Shredded native cedar is the best choice.

IVY IN TREES

Q. Our fifteen-year-old sweetgum tree has English ivy growing up into the tree from a bed beneath. Will this ivy growth be harmful to the tree in any way?

A. Vines on trees can look good but can also be a significant problem. If they climb high enough to cover the foliage, the tree is robbed of sunlight needed by the foliage to conduct photosynthesis and manufacture food for the root system. The stems of the vines on the trunks of the trees can also be a problem. The aging, enlarging woody growth expands with tremendous pressure and can break things when in tight places. This heavy stem growth can also hold moisture against the bark of the tree and lead to rot and decay. It's best to keep the vines on the ground. Even the ivy or any other ground covers around the base of the tree can hold too much moisture against the bark, causing rot. This condition can slowly girdle the tree.

LANTANA

Q. Quick question about lantanas. Had great luck this past year. The butterflies were everywhere. Now it is almost winter, and they still have green leaves. Do you pull them up and replant, or trim them back to the ground? They are facing southwest, with the house behind them, and they still have leaves, which are just a little browned on the edges. Thanks.

A. If your lantana is still hanging on, it would probably be best to go ahead and cut the plant back to a couple of inches from the ground and cover with a fluffy mulch such as leaves or shredded tree trimmings. Shredded native tree trimmings would be best, especially Eastern red cedar or mountain cedar. You will really appreciate the fragrance, pest resistance, and growth-enhancing qualities next growing season.

LIVING FENCES

Q. I live in the old part of Denton where 8-foot privacy fences look rather out of place. However, I want to screen my back yard from view from the street. The area where I want a living fence has competition from tree roots, although not for long—they are large hackberries on the decline. Please give me some suggestions of trees/shrubs that I can plant closely to screen my sons' sandbox and my compost pile. And, of course, I would love to feed the birds while I am at it. Love the organic way, and so do my sons, who love the worms and lizards that thrive in our garden!

A. I would use a mix of the following plants: eastern red cedar, yaupon holly, rusty blackhaw viburnum, Carolina buckthorn, and wax myrtle. These are all native plants and will provide a mix of evergreens, fall color, berries for birds, and interesting texture contrasts.

MAINTENANCE

Organic plant maintenance is based on the simple fact that if the soil is healthy and the plants are stress free, there will be few insect pests and diseases. Diseases that occasionally pop up can be controlled with baking soda, milk, neem, tea tree oil, and cornmeal. Insect pests can be controlled with garlic, pepper, orange oil, and diatomaceous earth. Yes, all foods.

MUSHROOMS

Q. I have a flower bed with ferns and hostas on the north side of my house. It doesn't receive much sun. The ferns are doing great, but I did have a problem with the pillbugs because it was so damp. I used the cayenne pepper, and things are getting better. I now have tons of mushrooms growing in the mulch. Are these going to hurt my ferns?

A. Those mushrooms are just the fruiting bodies of organic-matter-eating fungi. They do no harm to plants unless they grow heavily right at the stem and engulf small plants. They can be killed with baking soda or potassium bicarbonate spray, but it really isn't necessary.

NANDINAS

Nandinas should be pruned by following the longest shoots to the ground and cutting them off there. This technique effectively lowers the overall height but maintains the natural form of the plants. Shearing or boxing nandinas completely ruins their beauty and injures the health of the plants. It would be okay to do the nandina pruning in the summer, but the ideal time is in late winter.

PANSIES

Q. I've tried pansies for the last several years and have lost nearly all of them to pillbugs. I've used garlic tea, cayenne pepper, and diatomaceous earth to no avail. I can't keep up with the bugs. The products work when freshly applied, but if we have a rain, the bugs beat me to the pansies. They eat the stems at the base of the plants, which pretty much kills the plants.

A. Plant the pansies in full sun and apply a mix of equal amounts cedar flakes, natural diatomaceous earth, and hot pepper. Spray weekly with Garrett Juice plus garlic. Omit the garlic when the pests are under control. A mulch of shredded native cedar will also help.

Q. My front flower bed has wilting pansies. This spring I cultivated the bed and added lava sand, organic fertilizer, greensand, and earthworm castings and then planted petunias, which did great until the really hot days hit. The bed is covered with cedar bark mulch. This fall I just dug up around each plant I was transplanting and worked in some lava sand, earthworm castings, and organic fertilizer before planting. A few days after I planted, one of the plants was limp and wilted. Within a few days, it was dead. This has continued to happen, with no regularity or pattern. I have had a problem in this bed in the past with small snails. If it is snails, what should I do?

A. It could be fungal disease. For that, add cornmeal at about 20 pounds per 1,000 square feet. If slugs, snails, or pillbugs are the culprits, dust the surface of the soil with a mix of horticultural cedar flakes, natural diatomaceous earth, and crushed hot pepper. Spraying with the Garrett Juice mix and garlic tea will also help. You could also apply beneficial nematodes to control any of the soil-dwelling insect pests.

PERENNIALS

Q. When is the best time to transplant perennials? My sister has a perennial garden and wants to share her plants with me. She lives in central Arkansas, and her plants are three years old.

A. In general, the best time to divide or transplant is the season opposite the blooming period. For example, the spring-blooming perennials should be moved in the fall. Have the beds prepared first with compost, lava sand, Texas greensand, and cornmeal, and cover the bare soil with a shredded natural mulch after the perennials have been moved to their new homes.

PERIWINKLES

Q. We have a large bed of periwinkles. All of a sudden large patches of the flowers are dying. We pulled one plant up, and it looked as if the roots may have been eaten a little, but the stems were also brown. Do you have any idea what it might be?

A. It could be the fungal disease called *Phytophthora*. Next year, add cornmeal to the soil prior to planting and make sure the plants are in the full sun, especially in the morning, and don't plant them until the soil is good and warm in the late spring or early summer. Periwinkles also need very well-prepared and well-drained beds.

PETUNIAS

Q. All my petunias and unopened flower pods are being eaten up. The only insects that I have noticed around are roly-poly bugs. Could they be the culprit? We really enjoy your program and ideas. Someone actually complimented us on our lawn! That's a first.

A. Dust the ground under the plants with a mix of natural diatomaceous earth, hot pepper, and cedar flakes or horticultural cedar. The proportions are not important, but the DE should make up the largest percentage because it's the cheapest. This will also help with slugs and snails. A spray of garlic-pepper tea will also help.

PHOTINIAS

Q. I have a "hedge" of six 6-foot photinias that provides a beautiful backdrop to my backyard garden. The shrubs are constantly dogged with the leaf spot disease. I have sprayed for several seasons with Daconil, as recommended by the chemical guy. This year I have gone organic, so am not spraying the poison anymore. I aerated the soil around the photinias, as you suggested for the Sick Tree Treatment. However, to do the other things you suggest for that treatment would cost a considerable sum, as I have priced it at the organic store. The businessperson I am tells me it would be cheaper to let the photinias die if they do, and replant with a better native choice. But the homeowner in me will miss my photinias, especially the red color.

They have been sick for years, and I don't think there's any guarantee that after I do the Sick Tree Treatment they will live. It just seems wiser to let them go. If they die, I would like another hedge-type row of trees in their place. Would I be able to plant in the same place, or would the roots be so thick underground that they wouldn't let me plant something new?

A. You could cut the plants down and plant new material into the roots of the photinias, but my Sick Tree Treatment not only works, it is the most cost-effective approach available—for several reasons. First, the toxic chemical recommendations like Daconil and Bayleton don't work at all, as you have seen. They may slow down the disease pathogens for a short while, but they don't do anything helpful about the problem that caused the disease in the first place. They also kill off the beneficial microorganisms on the plant and in the soil, and that can lead to additional problems. My approach stimulates the helpful microbes, which makes the soil healthier and actually addresses the problem. Also, my solution works over the long term and eliminates the need to throw more money away every year on toxic pesticides. And finally, my approach usually works even in the short term, so your plants don't die and have to be replaced. Final note—even if your plants die after using my recommendations, your money hasn't been wasted. The next round of plants will love the soil improvements you have made. The toxic chemical poisons only have two uses—to make a profit for those selling the products and to sometimes temporarily keep sick plants alive for a little longer. They never solve the problems that created the pest invasion in the first place. If you replant, look at using a mix of plants, including Eastern red cedar, Nellie R. Stevens holly, and yaupon holly. Just move over to plant in between the photinia stumps, but add some additional cornmeal, wheat bran, and molasses first.

POISON IVY

Q. What do you recommend to use as a cure for poison ivy or poison oak? Thanks.

A. For the rash, comfrey juice right out of the stems and leaves of the big perennial herb works better than any store-bought medicines. To get rid of the plants, digging them out is the only practical answer in most cases. Several repeated sprays of strong vinegar with orange oil added will work if the spray can be kept off the desirable plants. Use 10 percent pickling vinegar or stronger and add 2 ounces orange oil or d-limonene per gallon. Add no water. There are several commercial products now available. The often recommended toxic chemical broadleaf herbicides such as 2,4-D and Trimec should not be used in the root systems of trees, or anywhere else for that matter.

PONDS

Q. I live on land with a 3-acre pond. I have been thinking about planting some trees on the levee that holds the water in. The levy is 10-plus feet wide at the top. Is it safe to plant trees near the water or anywhere on the dam itself? I've heard that trees could do damage to the levy.

A. Pond experts say that it's probably best to keep the trees away from dams because when roots die and rot, a void can be formed and a leak can result. That is the stance of the soil conservation people as well. I personally have seen hundreds of ponds and lakes with beautiful tree stands all over the dams. I guess it's your choice. A member of the Ground Crew recently reported an interesting observation. While driving across Texas during one of our summer droughts, it was obvious that ponds with trees around them had more water than bare ponds. The conclusion was that the evaporation lost water from ponds quicker than nearby trees could pull it out.

ROOTS AND POOL PLASTER

Q. Do you have a rule of thumb regarding building an in-ground gunite swimming pool in a yard with mature trees? We did just that and have questions about whether we made a good decision. Trees in question are live oak, cedar elm, and pecan. We live in north Dallas with clay soil, and over time and changing weather, the pool plaster has had various cracks. The wall area near the shallow-end skimmer has cracked, and there are actual roots peaking through the plaster. Is it possible for tree roots to penetrate a 12-inch-thick gunite wall? Or did the pool structure fail and the roots find their way to the water? Sort of the chicken and the egg situation depending on whether you're talking to the pool people or the tree arborist.

A. Sorry, but the only answer is that you got a sorry pool shell. There is no possible way that tree roots could break a well-built pool shell. This is usually my same answer to those who think that tree roots caused foundation problems. It just doesn't happen unless there is a serious fault in the engineering or quality of construction.

If the concrete structure of the pool is installed properly, roots from nearby trees will not be a problem. The only way roots could be growing through the gunite shell is if the concrete is flawed and cracked. In that case, the roots take advantage of the weakness and grow aggressively in the moist area created by the crack. I've worked around trees near pools for many years and have never seen the tree roots be the culprit.

SEASONAL COLOR

Q. I've got some flower beds that get no direct sunlight at all. I've been preparing the beds as described in your book. What plant suggestions do you have?

A. The best color in the shade for summer includes coleus, impatiens, caladiums, 'Big Blue' liriope, and purple wandering Jew. You can also plant the spring-flowering bulbs in shaded areas, but they might not return that well next year.

SOIL LEVELING AND ARMADILLOS

Q. We have three levels in our back yard down to a creek. I want to raise the second level to the height of the top level. There are trees on the second level, and it is about 5 feet lower. Will it hurt the trees to fill in the area around them with dirt? Also, how do you keep an armadillo from digging up a yard?

A. Yes, it will kill the trees. Covering tree roots with more than an inch or two of soil will shut off the gas transfer of oxygen in and carbon dioxide out. Building small rings around the trees is a total waste of money because there are very few feeder roots near the trunk. Although keeping soil off the bark of the tree will keep the bark from rotting, the roots will still be smothered. Trees covered with several feet of soil will definitely die. It may take five or more years, but the trees will die.

Trapping armadillos is the only answer. Ignore those who recommend treating for grubworms with diazinon or some other poison as a way to get the armadillos. Armadillos eat roots, many different kinds of insects, and earthworms. They also just like rooting around in the ground.

Q. I am planning on grading part of my back yard to alleviate the drastic slope. It is about 20–25 feet wide, and I plan on adding from 0 to about 18 inches of fill dirt or sandy loam. I plan on finishing with St. Augustinegrass sod. Currently there is some Bermudagrass and plenty of weeds. I heard one of your suggestions of newspaper to retard the growth of grass and weeds in flower beds. Would it be feasible to put down newspaper on top of the existing grass/weeds prior to covering with dirt? Do you think this would help keep the existing growth from coming up through the St. Augustine?

A. Bad plan—from two standpoints. Burying any living plant material will create a black muck layer in the soil that will be hard on plant roots for a long time. Also, some of the Bermudagrass will live and grow up to the surface to become a serious weed from now on. The existing vegetation should be completely removed by scraping it away and putting it in the compost pile prior to adding the fill.

SPRAYERS

Q. Could you pass along how to use Garrett Juice in an adjustable hose-end sprayer? We have sprayed once using a setting of ¼ teaspoon per gallon. Is that enough, using the juice straight from the container?

A. I don't recommend hose-end sprayers at all for foliar feeding or pest control spraying. You don't want a cheap piece of plastic doing the mixing. Hose-end sprayers are inconsistent in their mixing and stop up easily. I recommend devices that spray the mix that you have prepared. Pump-up sprayers are in this category, but the best choice is the trombone sprayer. It has a metal pump-action device and a rubber tube with a weight that goes into the bucket of spray mix. You can be comfortable that everything coming out of the nozzle is your precise mix. Trombone sprayers are easy to use, will cover large areas quickly, and are easy to clean up and store. For larger properties, the power sprayers function the same way. You can use my formula for ready-to-use Garrett Juice or follow the label directions on the commercial product. This advice applies to any organic spray.

STEEL EDGING

Q. What would be a good, preferably inexpensive, material for bordering a vegetable and herb garden area? I want to have it clearly designated from the rest of the yard and consist of raised beds.

A. The most cost-effective edging is steel curbing. The most practical, long-term edging is a concrete mowing strip or beam. If you go the steel route, don't use the flimsy stuff that bends when stepped on. Some of that weak material was accidentally installed in my landscaping, but it will be removed and replaced with ⅛-inch-by-4-inch material as soon as I have time. Some folks like to use brick or concrete blocks for edging, but I'm not a big fan of that idea either, because the grasses, especially Bermudagrass, grow through the cracks and become a big maintenance problem.

VINE CHOICES

Q. I would appreciate your suggestions for a vine selection to cover our newly constructed pergola. I don't have a bed from which to plant—the deck abuts a fence on one side and a sidewalk on the other. I'm resigned to plant something in pots and have it climb up/around columns to the overhead structure. The deck is 40 feet wide and faces east, so morning sun is strong, although it is shaded some by a large pecan tree in the back yard. Would mandevilla be a good selection? My local gardener suggested a Lady Banks rose, which is intriguing me, although I understand it has a relatively short bloom period. Another idea I have is to plant moonflowers and morning glories from seed, although that obviously offers nothing for winter months. My biggest concern is what size pots are appropriate and how best to prepare the soil so these plants are as healthy as possible and don't need to be repotted very often. I'm rather novice, but trying hard to go organic.

A. The answer to the pot size is bigger is better from the plant-health standpoint, but huge pots may not look good. Mandevilla is a good vine choice even though it is tropical. It does very well in pots during the summer. The morning glories and moonflowers would be fine as a secondary choice, but remember that they don't bloom till fall and are annuals. Lady Banks gets so big and wide, it would be okay but requires a lot of maintenance. Good permanent options are as follows: crossvine is a wonderful native evergreen with spring flowers in red and yellow; sweet autumn clematis is a late-summer white-flower bloomer that is bare in the winter; grape is a fast grower and has the advantage of summer fruit; trumpet vine is deciduous but has long-lasting summer flowers; passion vine is deciduous with dramatic summer flowers that are primarily purple, but other colors are available; Texas coral honeysuckle is the only honeysuckle I recommend (the others are weeds); and Carolina jessamine is an evergreen with yellow spring flowers.

VINE REMOVAL

Q. I have an old vine that I have been trying to kill, but the commercial products I have used have not done the job. Do you

**have any home remedy that I can try? I have spent $20.00, and it
is still alive.**

A. Sorry you wasted your money on toxic chemicals. Whatever
the vine is—it can be killed with either of two organic techniques.
Cutting the main trunk down flush with the ground is the first step
in either case. The best approach is to drill holes in the stump and
fill them with some organic material that will feed the microorganisms and rot the stump and roots. Drill the holes as big and deep
and close together as time allows. Fill the holes with sugar, molasses, old jellies or jams, buttermilk, or fertilizer. Moisten and cover
it all with a thick layer of shredded mulch. The second approach
is to cut the tree down and then spray the sucker shoots as they
emerge with an organic herbicide. Vinegar-based commercial
products are available, but you can make a homemade spray. Start
with full-strength 10 percent or 20 percent white vinegar. This is
not the same vinegar we use for amending the water for potted
plants and as an important ingredient in Garrett Juice. For those
purposes, use the 5 percent natural stuff such as apple cider vinegar. White distilled vinegar is fine for killing things. Add to the full-
strength vinegar about 2 ounces of orange oil or d-limonene per
gallon. No water should be added to the mix. After killing back the
sprouts for a while with this spray, the stored energy will be used
up from the roots, which will die and rot in the ground.

WEEDS

**Q. Help. I have neglected my garden this year, but now I have
time to do some repair. It's been overtaken by weeds—mostly
henbit and crabgrass. What can I do now to improve it and keep
my husband from using herbicides?**

A. It's a great time to begin the soil-building process, which
will help control the weeds next summer. Apply a humate product
now at about 10 pounds per 1,000 square feet. On or near March 1,
you should apply corn gluten meal at 20 pounds per 1,000 square
feet. The corn gluten meal will suffice as the first major fertilization
of the year. From that point forward, use the Basic Organic Program. Crabgrass wouldn't be growing during the dormant season,
and the henbit can be controlled by mowing it.

Q. We live in the country and have a very long gravel driveway. What's the best way to get rid of grasses and weeds? I pull them out year-round but have resorted to Roundup until now. I'd like to stop that, too, but can't have the grasses and weeds growing.

A. Weeds in gravel or cracks in concrete can be killed easily with the strong vinegar sprays, especially if mixed with citrus oil. Start with full-strength vinegar, 10 percent or 20 percent, and mix in 2 ounces of orange oil, other citrus oil, or d-limonene per gallon. Spray on a sunny, warm or hot day and watch grasses and broadleaf plants turn brown and shrivel. More than one spraying might be needed, same as is often the case with the toxic chemical products. Commercial products that contain versions of this mix include Weed Eraser, Garden-Ville Organic Weed Control, and Burn Out. One listener has reported that adding ¼ cup of salt to the vinegar makes the killing power more permanent. Just be careful with this idea. Salt can mess up the chemistry of the soil.

Trees

AMERICAN ELM

Q. I have a small grove of American elm. The area beneath the trees is overgrown with weeds and vines. I would like to eliminate the weeds without harming the trees. Could I till the top ½–1 inch of soil to loosen the vines and weeds without damaging the feeder roots? I then plan to follow with your recommended Sick Tree Treatment. Would spraying with dormant oil be appropriate, or would you recommend another preventative for the lacebug problem I've had the past two seasons? Finally, to prevent weed/vine regrowth I planned to supplement the mulch with a base of weed-block fabric or newspaper.

A. Almost all surface-fed roots will be destroyed by tilling. Surface roots are the most important roots because they do the most nutrient and water uptake, as well as oxygen intake. That's right— leaves take in carbon dioxide and give off oxygen, but roots take in oxygen and give off carbon dioxide. That exchange is critical to proper mineral uptake. The best weed control in tree roots is by hand, grubbing hoe, Japanese planting tool, or sharp shooter removal and the addition of a thick layer of mulch. Shredded tree trimmings are best; shredded native cedar is the ultimate choice. Pine bark is the worst choice because it won't stay in place and breaks down into a mucky material. Using the Sick Tree Treatment is a good idea—it would help the tree's immune system and reduce the lacebug attack in the summer. If the insect problem persists this first summer while the root system is improving, drench the root zone with one of the neem products, and follow my normal recommendations in the Basic Organic Program.

BALD CYPRESS

Q. **How do I tell, not only with my bald cypress but with any plant, whether I'm giving too much or too little water? Do yellow or brown leaves always mean too little water?**

A. No, not necessarily. To be absolutely sure, get one of the yellow fiberglass probes that irrigation people use. There are no dials or gauges on the probe. Just the feel of one stab into the ground will give you the answer. If the probe goes in the ground easily and sounds like a cow pulling her foot out of the mud when removing, the soil's too wet. If the probe won't go into the ground at all, it's too dry. Last point—bald cypress can grow well in moist to wet soil but not in the dry soil, especially in droughty summers.

Q. **How do I make soil acid for bald cypress tree planting?**

A. Bald cypress trees will grow in the black clay alkaline soils. The shallow white rock is the condition to avoid. Most of the trees come from deep sandy-soil areas. To improve the high pH soil so that bald cypress and other chlorosis-prone plants will fare well, apply one of the commercial humates at about 10 pounds per 1,000 square feet, lava sand at 80 pounds, Texas greensand at 80 pounds, cornmeal at 20 pounds, and if possible, a shredded cedar mulch layer.

BRADFORD PEARS

Q. **I have two seven-year-old Bradford pears and one Shumard red oak. I would like to level the yard and need about 4–6 inches of material to do this. What can I use that will not hurt the trees?**

A. Adding 2 inches of soil to the root zone of trees will hurt them—4–6 inches will really hurt them. The damage comes from a smothering action. Feeder roots near the surface of the soil are sensitive to most changes, but filling is arguably the most damaging. It fouls up the proper gas transfer—oxygen in and carbon dioxide out. The result is death of beneficial microorganisms, especially the root-colonizing mycorrhizal fungi that are critical to the health of trees. Filling can be done effectively and safely with compost or with core aeration. The plugs removed from the soil in the high areas can be raked down into the low areas to do a home-made job of cutting and filling.

BUR OAK FUNGUS

Q. Yesterday while I was feeding liquid seaweed to my bur oak in the front yard, I noticed a small area of bright yellow material in the hardwood mulch under the tree. I assumed a dog had gotten sick and thought nothing more about it. This morning, the yellow material had expanded to the size and thickness of a large sponge. I realize this is some type of mold or fungus, but I was wondering if it was harmful to either the tree or humans and if I should take steps to remove it.

A. Nothing to worry about. That is just a beneficial fungus helping to break down the organic matter. If it bothers you, stir it up with a cultivating tool or spray it with potassium bicarbonate at 1 rounded tablespoon per gallon of water. Mushrooms should be handled the same way.

CHINESE PISTACHIO

Q. What is the normal life span of the Chinese pistachio tree? I have planted a lot of trees in the last twenty years around my place in black and white soil. My new bur oaks really took a beat-ing this summer. They've lost leaves, and some may die. I also have four Chinese pistachio trees. I wasn't able to water this year. The Chinese pistachios did not seem to be affected by the heat and lack of water. They look great. I think this is the tree for this coun-try. They are growing fast and look good. Also, I am convinced I would have lost a lot of trees except for the cedar mulch. I have about 8 inches of cedar around my trees. In the spring, the high-way department trims all the cedars along the roads and grinds it up, and I haul it home and stockpile it. Thanks.

A. The cedar mulch and pistachio trees are important tools for us North Texas gardeners. Bur oaks are, too. Even though yours look bad now, they will probably be okay. Many trees, including bur oaks, kick off leaves in the summer to compensate for the lack of water in the soil. If the soil dryness was too severe or lasted too long, the trees could be permanently injured. All you can do is wait and see. Chinese pistachio does behave much like a drought-tolerant native Texas tree even though it hails from the Orient. I've only noticed two common problems—one is "wet feet" caused by overwatering or poor drainage. The second is a structural problem. Young Chinese pistachios often have a weak trunk system that branches into two equal vertical shoots. As these twins grow, they form a weak "crotch" that is V shaped. The problems resulting from this flawed connection don't usually show up until the tree has developed a large top and is looking great in the landscape. It's then that the V splits right down the middle of the trunk and breaks the tree in half. This condition can also affect other kinds of trees, and the solution is the same in all cases. While the tree is still young, remove one or the other half. Try to save the strongest half even though they will appear to be near matches. Yes, the young tree will look awkward for a while—young Chinese pistachios usually do anyway—but the tree will fill out and regain its symmetry before you know it.

CHINKAPIN OAK

Q. I have a chinkapin oak, planted late last year. The leaves are yellow and some of the leaf growth is on the trunk. I started watering once a week for nine minutes when we were receiving rain. Now I water twice a week for nine minutes. Last month I started deep watering the tree for an extra fifteen minutes. Regardless of more or less water, the leaves remain yellow. The soil is clay and limestone.

A. I can't give you a specific watering schedule—it depends on soil structure, slope, and other factors. Probe into the soil to see what's really going on, and adjust the water as needed. If you haven't already, apply the Sick Tree Treatment.

CHLOROSIS

Q. I have a tree that was diagnosed with chlorosis. The arborist said it is a non-native variety of red oak growing in strongly alkaline soil. He thought it would be too difficult to change the pH of my entire yard, even using greensand, etc. It is not a big tree, and he said it would be best to cut it down and replant a native variety that is accustomed to the high-calcium Texas soil. Does that sound reasonable?

A. I agree with your tree guy in this case. The only thing you might try first is the Sick Tree Treatment.

CHRISTMAS TREE CARE

Q. We just bought a live Christmas tree and are wondering what liquid solution we should give it to keep it healthy until December 25. Just water? Compost tea? Garrett Juice? I am also filling the tree stand with tap water every morning. It takes about 20 ounces to fill every morning. Am I giving too much water, or not enough? The tree is about 7 feet tall.

A. I think tap water works as well as anything. Just add as much as the tree will suck up. No more, no less. I tried one of the magic mixes one year and all I accomplished was a mess when the mucky stuff spilled on the floor.

DROUGHT-TOLERANT TREES

Q. What are some of the most popular drought-tolerant native species trees for Texas? Also, for a St. Augustine yard in light of the drought, should we fertilize now or wait, and with what?

A. Some of the best drought-tolerant trees are bur oak, Texas red oak, Texas ash, cedar elm, Eve's necklace, chinkapin oak, and Lacey oak. Summer is an excellent time to fertilize with one of the gentle organic fertilizers such as Garden-Ville, GreenSense, Bradfield, Maestro-Gro, Alliance, and Bioform. The analysis of these products will range from 1-1-1 to 7-2-2, but all should be applied at 20 pounds per 1,000 square feet. The organic approach is to feed the soil and stimulate the growth-beneficial microorganisms. The healthy soil feeds the plants slowly, naturally, and completely.

LIGHTNING DAMAGE

Q. Lightning hit my "blackjack" tree and took all the bark off 4 feet up and all the way around the circumference of the tree. Is there anything we can do to save it?

A. Got bad news. In a heavy rainstorm, lightning usually goes down, or up as some say, the moisture on the bark of the tree. It scars the tree by ripping a line of bark off, but the tree normally lives. But when the lightning goes through the center of the tree, it's a different story. The result is an explosion of bark coming off all around the tree. The entire cambium layer is destroyed, and the tree dies.

LIVE OAKS

Q. Six weeks ago we transplanted two live oaks and one red oak tree on our property—followed your instructions as to transplanting trees. One of the live oaks has lost most of its leaves, but the others did not. Is the loss of leaves something that I should be concerned about, or is this a situation that sometimes happens?

A. When live oaks lose their leaves in the late winter, it is not anything to worry about. All trees, including the evergreens, drop their leaves once a year at least. Live oaks push their old leaves off as the buds swell in the late winter or early spring. Sometimes the new spring leaves form right away, but other times the trees remain bare for a while. When live oak leaves are turning yellow brown and releasing easily from the tree, that's generally a perfectly natural condition. On the other hand, if the leaves turn solid brown and refuse to release easily when tugged, that is a bad sign. Your tree may already be dead.

Live Oak Drippings

Q. Can you tell me why my live oak tree is leaving a saplike cover on my vehicles? It used to not do this. It just started about

one to two months ago. I have noticed a lot of bees and flies around it.

A. Sounds like the sticky honeydew from aphids. Spray the foliage with molasses water (1 ounce of molasses per gallon of water) and release ladybugs on the tree. Next apply the Sick Tree Treatment to improve the plant's immune system so the aphids won't be attracted to the tree in the first place. It is usually a temporary problem, so you could just park somewhere else for a while.

Live Oak Roots

Q. One of our live oak trees has very large roots on the top of the ground. What can we do about the roots? It is hard to walk in the front yard.

A. Roots can be pruned the same as limbs, with minimal damage if the work is done in the fall or winter and you don't sever more than about 20 percent of the tree's root system. The other approach is to change from grass to ground cover in that area, with stepping stones maybe, so no roots have to be cut. Although the tree will probably survive, all cuts—to the roots or to the top growth—hurt the tree. Pruning is done for your benefit, not the tree's. Another solution is to cover the problem area with shredded mulch or decomposed granite.

MIMOSAS AND CARPENTER ANTS

Q. We recently had our mimosa and fruitless mulberry trees trimmed. The man said we had carpenter ants in both of them and they were keeping the nutrients from getting up into the tree. He said the large leaves pointed to that also. What treatment should I use?

A. You need to get another tree company. That's the most bizarre sales pitch for unnecessary tree pruning and pest control I've ever heard—and I've heard plenty. Carpenter ants carve out dead and decaying wood to create their nests. They feed on living and dead insects, plant sap, honeydew from insects, pollen, and seed. They do not eat healthy tissue in trees or cause any injury whatsoever. Carpenter ants are opportunistic and take advantage of decaying and dead wood in trees that is caused by other factors. The most likely cause of problems in these two trees is weak genetics. They are both short-lived trash trees with weak immune systems. What will help these trees live longer is soil and root improvement. The Sick Tree Treatment is in order. If it doesn't save them, they can't be saved. See the Appendix.

MISTLETOE

Q. Is there any organic way to clean mistletoe from an elm tree without having to cut all of it out?

A. Nope. Trim it out and use the Sick Tree Treatment. Trees with strong immune systems will definitely resist the parasite to some degree. Poor-quality trees and those that have been assaulted with synthetic fertilizers and pesticides are the most susceptible to this parasite and other pests.

Q. I've heard that mistletoe can now be used as a fire ant control. I'd like to learn more about this.

A. All I know is that if you chop it up and sprinkle the fresh green pieces on the mounds, the ants seem to go away. I'm not at all sure exactly what happens, but it seems like a good natural way to control the pests, since we have so much mistletoe in the trees to get rid of. In case you haven't noticed, the population of this aerial parasitic seems to be on the increase. That probably relates to the overall decline in the health of our trees.

MULBERRIES AND NEW TREES

Q. We would like to plant oak seedlings near the declining mulberries so that they can be growing while the mulberries are around to still give us a little shade. Then we'd like to cut the mulberry trees down so the oaks can take over. (1) How close to the existing mulberry trees can we plant the oak seedlings; (2) how tall can we let the oaks get before we take out the mulberries, assuming they live several more years; and (3) should we plant the potted oaks now in the fall or wait until winter?

A. The small trees need to be planted far enough away from the mulberries to provide almost a full day of direct sun. Morning sun is especially important. As I always recommend, dig a very wide hole, backfill with the native soil only, and forget about the staking, wrapping, and thinning, as is often incorrectly recommended. The wide hole is even more important than usual in this case, since it will remove the large tree's competitive roots in that area and give the small trees an unoccupied space in which to develop. Plant the small trees right away, and cut the big tree down whenever you are ready to make the switch. Trees have a spurt of root growth in the fall and early winter. That will help the small trees take off with aggressive growth next spring.

PECANS

Q. Could you give me some tips on transplanting pecan trees? I have a small grove of six native pecan trees and would like to transplant a few of the seedlings that have come up. A couple of them are only 2–3 feet tall, and some are 7–8 feet tall. Since the pecan tree has a tap root, how far down do I have to dig? Obviously, I can't dig deep enough to get all the tap root. Can I dig down about 2–3 feet and then cut the tap root?

A. Two feet is probably deep enough, even for the tall trees. Be sure to dig a wide, rough-sided or square hole, backfill with nothing but the soil from the hole, settle the soil with water (no tamping), cover the disturbed area with a 50/50 mix of lava sand and compost (about 1 inch), then cover that with 3–5 inches of shredded tree-trimming mulch (native cedar is the best). Do this work soon, while the trees are still dormant. Do not thin out or cut back the top. Do not wrap the trunk. Do not stake the tree. And do not apply any form of synthetic fertilizer or root stimulator.

Q. What kind of pecan trees should I plant for sandy areas— 'Stuart,' 'Mohawk,' 'Shawnee,' 'Burkett,' 'Kiowa,' 'Pawnee,' 'Choctaw,' 'Desirable,' 'Wichita', or 'Cheyenne'? I am concerned with hardy growth and kernel quality. Also, how far apart should they be planted?

A. Don't plant any of those varieties. Texas A&M has even come around to recommending the trees that have small nuts. Plant natives or other small-nut trees such as 'Caddo,' 'Kansa,' or native seedlings at 40–50 feet on center. Pecan trees with small pecans have fewer insect and disease infestations and higher-quality meat, plus the trees get larger, live longer, and look better year after year.

Q. My five-year-old pecan tree in my back yard has two problems. The bark in several locations on the main trunk and limbs is flaking off. Also there are two places where the trunk and one major limb are cracking open.

A. I don't think you have a big problem—just use the organic pecan and fruit tree program in the Basic Organic Program. Bark sloughing off is common for pecan trees and indicates the tree is growing well. You might want to treat the cracked place with the Tree Trunk Goop. Mix equal amounts of natural diatomaceous earth, soft rock phosphate, and manure compost; add water; and slop it on the crack.

Pecan Grafting

Q. I have over a hundred grown pecan trees on my land in Sulphur Springs. The main problem is some of them produce what we call hog pecans. Because they are so small, only the feral hogs will bother with them. Where can I learn to graft paper shell onto my native pecan trees? My second question is: I saved about 150 pecans off one of my better trees to try to plant this spring, so how do I prepare the pecans so they will sprout and grow?

A. I recommend the hard-shell small pecans because the quality of the meat and oil is much higher than that of the large paper-shell varieties. A&M has even reversed its stand and now recommends the small-nut varieties instead of the large, paper-shell hybrids. Save your money and time. You'll have better-quality nuts and trees. To plant the native trees from pecans, put the nuts in the garden soil or in potting soil as soon as they fall from the trees. The depth should be 1–2 times the length of the nut. Keep the soil moist but not sopping wet, and watch out for squirrels digging up the pecans. Wire mesh or gravel can sometimes help.

PINES

Q. What type of pine tree would grow best in Richardson, Texas?

A. Probably Austrian pine, but the native eastern red cedar would be a better choice. By the way, don't listen to those who recommend Japanese black pine. They are dying all over North Texas. Yes, I used to recommend them, too. The only really safe place to plant pine trees in North Texas is in the red sandy bands that run through the black and white soils.

Q. **Home Depot is selling a tree tagged as "Texas Afghan pine,"** *Pinus eldarica.* **Can you give me any information about it?**

A. *Pinus eldarica,* also known as Afghan or Mondell pine, is native to the Caucasus Mountains of Afghanistan, southern Russia, and Pakistan. It's hardly a native Texan. Being a desert tree gives it a major fatal flaw. Long rainy periods or overwatering will kill this tree by stimulating root fungal diseases. It does very well in West Texas and other areas of low rainfall.

POST OAKS

Q. **Our home was built in 1984 and has two old post oaks 4–5 feet in diameter on the edge of the property. Both trees were disturbed during construction, and several feet of soil was back-filled over their root systems. They are showing major signs of distress. An arborist recommended I uncover the trunks down to the root flares and treat the distressed post oaks with powdered root hormone in holes drilled in the soil under the canopy. Do you think that would help?**

A. Sounds like a pretty good plan, but I prefer the entire Sick Tree Treatment after returning the grade to its original level. It will also help if you plant only native, low-water-requiring plants like the community that would have existed prior to development. Take a look at horseherb, snakeroot, frog fruit, coralberry, inland seaoats, agarita, rusty blackhaw viburnum, and Carolina buckthorn. Post oaks are very fragile—good luck!

Q. **I have several acres of post oaks, with an occasional bur oak and cedar elm. My research has revealed that these post oaks are extremely sensitive to soil changes (primarily compaction), and I am nervous about planting underneath them. I have heard you recommend coralberry, horseherb, and several other natives, and was wondering what type of soil preparation is allowable under** such a seemingly fragile tree. Is tilling in organic matter going to do irreparable damage to tree roots? Will too much mulch do harm? Also, some of the leaves are developing small round holes covering much of the leaf. Other leaves have developed a brown skeleton look—like a web or gauze appearance.

A. You're right—these native trees are very sensitive to soil changes and root damage. Tilling and heavy bed preparation is definitely hard on the trees. Plus the native plants you mentioned don't need the improvements. Dig wide, rough-sided holes and backfill with the existing soil—as in planting trees. You might also try some inland seaoats and agarita. Mulch with a thin layer (½ inch) of compost and then a 2-inch layer of shredded native tree trimmings. The holes in the leaves are minor damage from various insects. That symptom will clear up when the roots are more healthy and the tree is happier.

Q. I live in Euless, Texas, on a 2-acre wooded lot populated primarily with mature post oaks of varying sizes from 5- to 16-inch trunk diameters. Over the last three years I've lost a dozen or more trees to a disease I've not seen before and am quite concerned that I'll lose more trees. The symptom is that the tree loses its bark and dies. If inspection is made soon after the bark falls off or if some is pulled off, the underlying wood is covered with a dark-chocolate-colored powder. After the bark falls off, the remaining bare wood becomes a kind of sooty gray color. I've noticed that my neighbors also have trees dying with the same symptoms.

A. Sounds like a fungal disease called hypoxolyn canker. It can be controlled with the Sick Tree Treatment unless the roots have already died back too far. These are diseases that attack trees with weakened immune systems. The recent drought is one of the problems, but the overuse of synthetic fertilizers and herbicides can also be part of the problem.

Q. We live in a house built about eighteen months ago, and there are many post oak trees in the yard. About eight of the trees seem to be dying during this summer heat. Is there any hope for restoring the trees to life? I have heard that deep watering and root stimulators may help. Are these good techniques to use?

A. Post oaks have several problems. They don't like people

for one thing, and the severe droughts in 1998 and 1999 crippled many trees in North Texas. Most arborists and scientists refer to this disease as a problem, but it is actually only a symptom. Hypoxolyn cankers occur on stressed trees only. This fungus is a common microorganism on most trees and is no problem to healthy ones. However, it can severely injure or kill trees weakened by environmental factors such as drought, root disease, mechanical injury, overfertilizing, herbicide and other pesticide use, or construction activities. The disease organisms move into the conducting tissue of the trunk and limbs and produce the cankers. These abnormal growths are activated by reduced moisture in the plant, caused by the failure of the root system to bring water up properly. To spot this disease, look for severe injuries on branches or the trunk. Crown dieback is another common symptom. Patches of bark often slough off the trunk and limbs of infested trees, revealing the fungi's fruiting bodies. Later, the sapwood turns dull yellow with black lines. Powdery greenish, brown, or gray masses of the spores appear on the surface of the crusty, fungal patches in the early part of the growing season.

Hipoxylon canker can attack post, southern red, white, water, and blackjack oak and sometimes hickory. As with all diseases, the key is prevention. Protect trees during construction, avoid herbicides and pesticides, and minimize site changes, especially those that impact the root zones of trees. Select the appropriate tree species, and plant them using the Natural Way planting techniques.

It's difficult to save trees showing fruiting structures of hypoxolyn, but try by carefully pruning branches that have the fungal patches and then apply the Sick Tree Treatment. Organic root stimulators such as seaweed and compost tea are excellent, but I do not recommend the commonly referred to synthetic products that are very high in artificial forms of phosphorous. Deep watering is a good idea as long as the drainage is adequate.

PRUNING

Q. I am just getting started in organics. I have quite a few dead limbs in some large trees in my yard. They are 40–60-foot oaks

and sweetgums. I know they should be removed, but the estimate I got to remove them was $600.00. Is that reasonable? Will it hurt the tree to just let the limbs fall off naturally?

A. Not at all—that's what happens in the forest. The only urgency related to removal of dead, diseased, or injured limbs comes from risk of injury to people, pets, and structures if the limbs fall. You'll have to make that call. Dead limbs actually provide habitat for beneficial microbes, insects, and other animals.

Q. You always say don't prune trees. Do you mean fruit trees also?

A. It's okay to prune trees if a change is needed. I just don't want people fooled into thinking that regular pruning is needed for the health of the trees. Fruit trees are pruned, for example, to encourage large fruit and make picking easier—both for your benefit—not the trees'. Pruning shade trees to allow more light through so you can plant below or to remove limbs that are in the way is again for your benefit. Occasionally, corrective pruning is needed, but it's rare. Remove limbs that are rubbing, creating weak V crotches, or weighing the tree in an awkward fashion, but understand that annual thinning is not good for trees, "topping" or "cutting back" is barbaric, and "dehorning" is, or should be, criminal.

REDBUD TRANSPLANTS

Q. I have two young volunteer redbud trees in my flower bed. I would like to transplant them this fall or next spring. Both are about 3–4 feet tall but are not branched out. How do I make them branch out and have a good shape?

A. The only way to get trees to fill out better is to give them the proper conditions (sun, soil, drainage, etc.) and keep them healthy by using the organic techniques. Pruning doesn't help at all. It's always best for the health of trees to leave as much foliage as possible. The more foliage a plant has, the more sunlight can be collected for the manufacture of food.

ROYAL PAULOWNIA

Q. "Royal Paulownia smothered in lavish masses of bouquets of breathtaking lavender blue blooms!" The flyer/brochure says it will grow in virtually any soil. Please advise.

A. This mail-order plant has many common names—royal Paulownia, princess tree, empress tree, Karri, and foxglove tree. Even though I usually advise people to avoid these plants from ads that grossly exaggerate their benefits, this tree interests me, if we could just get some local growers to provide it. There is one in Highland Park that I pass occasionally that is about 25 feet tall and gorgeous when in bloom. Planting no more than one as an experiment might be fun, but I can promise more long-term beauty and success with the native flowering trees Mexican plum, desert willow, chitalpa, and Eve's necklace, as well as the versatile (though not native) crape myrtle, which comes to us from Asia.

SHANTUNG MAPLE

Q. Do you have an opinion about a maple tree called a Shantung maple? I just bought one, but they have not delivered it yet. It is supposed to have nice orange fall color. I would appreciate any feedback you can give me or if you can direct me to a good source of information. Also, do you have a recommendation for a red fall-color tree that does well in North Texas? Ultimate size would ideally be the size of a Caddo maple.

A. Dr. Carl Whitcomb has convinced me they are great trees. Shantung maple seems to be an excellent choice, but it has only been grown here a short time. I'd give it a shot. I have planted one at my office, and the initial growth is impressive. It will just about double the growth of the Caddo maple. For red foliage in shade trees, check out Chinese pistachio, Texas ash, Drummond red maple, and sweetgum. Chinese pistachio and Texas ash will grow in any soil as long as the drainage is sufficient. The red maple and sweetgum trees need deep soil. Rock of any color near the surface gives these trees problems.

SHUMARD RED OAK

Q. I live in south Arlington, which has heavy clay soil. Four to five years ago, I planted a 10–12-foot Shumard oak from a 10-gallon container. That same year I planted a red oak from an acorn. Except for an initial feeding when I planted them, the only feeding they get is when I do the entire yard. Guess which tree is bigger now? The red oak! Both are about 15–17 feet tall, with the red oak slightly taller. The container tree also had some insects on the foliage. The seedling-grown tree didn't. Why is the container tree not growing as fast as the other one? Is it a slower tree anyway? Also, the top 4 feet of this tree leans—what do I do there?

A. Both trees are red oaks, but your comparison is helpful in illustrating two points. First, the little tree grown from seed has never had its root system damaged. The container-grown tree could have had trauma more than once. It was probably grown as a seedling, then transplanted into the potting soil and container. When planted in the soil, the roots had to re-acclimate to a different soil again. The tree will probably be fine, but the red oak grown from seed in the same soil is happier and in less stress and therefore grows faster. The second point is that there's a good chance the container-grown tree was fertilized with soluble, synthetic fertilizer. Too much of the fake stuff can promote weak, unhealthy growth. That could explain the weak trunk. Don't stake the leaning tree. That's the worst thing you can do. Just continue to fertilize around the trees with the gentle organic fertilizers and add some lava sand and Texas greensand. The trunk will strengthen, and it won't take long for the tree to develop a beautiful, symmetrical appearance. There's one more possible cause to inspect. Make sure the container-grown tree is not planted too deep and doesn't have circling roots. If the tree is low, dish the area above the ball and leave the root ball exposed except for a thin layer of shredded mulch.

SICK TREE TREATMENT

Because I've gotten so many questions about various tree problems, I thought it would be a good time to give you an update on the Sick Tree Treatment. Many of the questions relate to Arizona and green ash and other poorly adapted trees that have lots of dead wood, curled leaves, and dripping sticky stuff. The shiny, sticky stuff is the honeydew from the aphids that are sucking the leaf juice and causing the leaf deformities.

Oak wilt is one of the most serious tree problems in Texas. It is a devastating disease of native and introduced red oaks and live oaks. The Texas Forest Service has been working on the problem for several years and recommends a program of trenching to separate the roots of sick trees from those of healthy trees and injection of a chemical fungicide called Alamo. I don't recommend this program and have a different proposal.

To look at this problem from a little bit different angle, let's consider the insect that's blamed. The nitidulid or sap-feeding beetle, the alleged culprit, feeds on tree sap in the spring and spreads the disease. Adult beetles look like tiny June bugs. They inhabit the fungal mats beneath the bark of diseased red oaks (*Quercus texana* and *Quercus shumardii*). Infectious beetles emerge from the fungal mats and deposit oak wilt spores in wounds on healthy trees by feeding on sap. These are the same insects that feed on rotting fruit in the orchard.

There is research evidence now that sapsuckers attack and drill holes in trees that are in stress. The stress causes sweeter and more concentrated sugars. The sap beetles are probably attracted to trees in a similar way. But even if the little beetles go to both healthy and weak trees, why do some trees succumb to the disease and some don't? Even if the beetles don't infect every tree, the roots reach far out and touch the surrounding tree roots. All the experts agree that the disease can easily spread through the roots. Even though the oak wilt disease has killed thousands of live oaks and red oaks in Texas, the disease can be stopped by using organic techniques. The plan is simple. Keep trees in a healthy condition so their immune system can resist the infection and disease. It has been noticed by many farmers and ranchers that the disease doesn't bother some trees—especially those that are mulched and those where the natural habitat under them has been maintained.

There's only experimental evidence so far, but we have seen excellent results from the following organic program:

1. Aerate the root zone heavily. Start between the dripline and the trunk and go far out beyond the dripline. A 7–12-inch depth of the aeration holes is ideal, but any depth is beneficial. An alternative is to spray the root zone with a microbe product such as Bio-Inoculant or AgriGro. Treating the root zone with a mycorrhizal fungus product such as Plant Health Care is also beneficial.

2. Apply Texas greensand at about 80 pounds per 1,000 square feet, lava sand at about 80 pounds per 1,000 square feet, cornmeal at about 20 pounds per 1,000 square feet, and sugar or dry molasses at about 5 pounds per 1,000 square feet. Cornmeal is a natural disease fighter, and sugar is a carbon source to feed the microbes in the soil.

3. Apply a 1-inch layer of compost, followed by a 3–5-inch layer of shredded native tree trimmings. Native cedar is the very best source for mulch. Do not pile mulch onto trunks.

4. Spray the foliage monthly or more often if possible with Garrett Juice (see formula in the Appendix). For large-scale farms and ranches, a one-time spraying is beneficial if the budget doesn't allow ongoing sprays. Adding garlic tea to the spray is also beneficial while the tree is in trouble.

5. Stop using high-nitrogen fertilizers and toxic chemical pesticides. The pesticides repel or kill the beneficial fungi, nematodes, and insects. The fake fertilizers are destructive to the important mycorrhizal fungi on the roots.

A premix of lava, greensand, and compost is now available from the organic suppliers. It is called Garden-Ville Sick Tree Treatment. All you'll have to add is cornmeal and topdressing mulch.

Since the fungal mats form on red oaks only, not on live oaks, the live oak wood can be used for firewood without any worry of spreading the oak wilt disease. Red oak wood needs to be stacked in a sunny location and covered with clear plastic to form a greenhouse effect to kill the beetles and fungal mats. When oaks are shredded into mulch, the aeration kills the pathogens and eliminates the possibility of disease spread. That goes for all species.

Is this nitidulid beetle the only way the problem could be spread? I doubt it. How about mechanical damage to tree trunks, wind, squirrels, hail, sapsuckers, and other birds and insects. Fire ants seem to prefer weaker trees over others and could be part of the spreading problem.

My recommended program has not yet been proven by any university and probably won't be even though the evidence continues to stack up. Improving the health of the soil, and thus the population of beneficial fungi on the root system, seems to be paramount. Spraying the foliage during the rebuilding of the soil and root system provides trace minerals to the plant that can't yet come in through the roots. This program is not just for oak wilt. It works for most environmental tree problems and all tree types. My point here is that if it works for oak wilt, it will work even more effectively for less deadly tree conditions. If your tree problem is a result of poor variety selection, I can only help you in the future. Choose more wisely next time.

For any physical damage to trunks, spray with hydrogen peroxide and then treat wounds with Tree Trunk Goop.

STAKING TREES

Q. My father planted six pine trees three years ago. He tied them from three points to posts for support. After the first year of growth, he started trying to untie them after they reached approximately 7–10 feet tall. When he took off the support ropes, every one of the trees bent almost to the ground. They seem to have good root systems and their trunks appear to be growing normally, but they are just like rubber. We cannot take the ropes off and don't know what to do. We live two miles across the Red River in Oklahoma in loamy soil. What can we do?

A. Now you know why I don't recommend staking trees. Staking tricks the tree. With something artificial holding the tree straight, the young tree doesn't develop the proper tensile strength in the trunk. Tree movement caused by the wind is very important. Obviously there are exceptions, but in general, trees should not be staked. When young trees are staked, they become dependent on the supports. There is only one option. Remove the stakes, accept the rubbery, bent-over look, and be patient. The trees will eventually develop the proper trunk strength and become beautiful trees, although having crooked trunks, which I think are interesting. Next time, start with stout trees that aren't staked and don't add your own. You might want to talk to those who are still advising tree staking—maybe they'll help you buy some new plants.

STUMP REMOVAL

Q. A friend of mine told me that you had a method of stump removal or rotting away of stumps. Since I have a couple of years to wait, I decided to give your method a try. What I was told is that you drill a hole in the stump and fill this hole with molasses and something else.

A. There really isn't any magic formula. Any kind of sugar or nitrogen product will do the trick. Start by drilling holes in the stump. Make the holes as large and deep and closely spaced as possible. Fill the holes with sugar, molasses, syrup, old jellies or jams, candies, buttermilk, or fertilizer of any kind. This is a good place to use up any of that synthetic fertilizer you might still have around the place, although organic fertilizer would certainly be better. Next, wet the stump and additions, and then cover it all with a thick layer of shredded mulch. How long the rotting takes depends on what kind of tree it is. Bois d'arc will take the longest to rot using this or any other technique. A more practical approach for some people is to hire a tree-care company to grind the stump out mechanically. It's quick, always successful, and doesn't cost much.

SWEETGUMS

Q. I have two sweetgum trees, both about eleven years old. One of them seems to be having a problem; half of the tree leaves are a much lighter green than the other half. They also have burned or browned tips. The other tree is a dark green and shows no problems. Could you help me with some ideas on the tree?

A. The most common sweetgum problem relates to soil. Sweetgums grow naturally in the sandy acid soils of East Texas and Oklahoma. They can adapt well to the heavy clay soils of North Texas but cannot adapt to the white rock that hides under the black alkaline soils. Iron additions are often recommended, but magnesium is the more common missing link in these soils. Sometimes chlorotic trees can be returned to health by applying humate and Texas greensand. Even if you apply the missing elements with the correct amendments, the roots will continue to grow beyond the treated area, and the symptoms of discolored leaves will return. If lots of compost and Texas greensand don't bring the tree back to the proper color, the best choice for the long term is to remove the tree and replace it with a more adaptable plant. Large-growing trees that can tolerate the high-calcium, alkaline soils include bur oak, chinkapin oak, Texas ash, Texas red oak, and cedar elm.

TRANSPLANTING TREES

Q. What is the proper way to dig trees up and replant them, either in a pot or grow bag, or in another area of our ranch? I have some 1–2-inch caliper Mexican plums, flameleaf sumac, red oaks, and Carolina buckthorn that I would like to place around my house.

A. Those native trees can be dug and transplanted from the wild with fair success. The key is to do the work in the fall and use the Natural Way planting techniques. Trees need about 9 inches of earth ball per caliper inch of trunk measured about 12 inches above the ground. Use large nails to pin burlap snugly around the ball to keep it firmly intact during the move. Just as when planting a new tree, the preparation of the new hole is important. It should be 1–2 inches less deep than the height of the ball. Measure— don't guess. It's better to underdig than to overdig the hole. If backfill needs to be added under the ball, the tree can settle and die from drowning. The width and shape of the hole is critical. The worst hole is one that has smooth sides, is round, and is just barely large enough to receive the tree ball. The best tree hole is large and ugly. I like wide, rough-sided, saucer-shaped holes. Big square-shaped holes are also good. Smooth, round holes encourage roots to circle and avoid growing out into the native soil. The circling will always injure the roots and often kill the tree. Death can result from root strangulation or from drying out. Severely circling roots prevent water from getting into the ball. This is an even greater problem with container-grown plants that already have circling roots.

Backfill should be the soil from the hole—period. No other material should be added—no peat moss, no bark, no foreign soil, no sand, no fertilizer or anything else. In solid-rock areas, use native soil from a nearby location, but it's okay to mix some broken rock into the backfill. Settle the soil with water. Tamping is bad because it can both push the oxygen out and cause large air pockets in the backfill. Adding some Garrett Juice or other fish and seaweed product to the backfill water will function as a mild organic root stimulator. Mycorrhizal fungi is also beneficial to add.

When the backfill is settled and level with the surrounding grade, apply a ½–1-inch layer of compost or earthworm castings to the disturbed area. Toss down enough volcanic rock such as lava sand to cover the same area, and then cover it all with a 3-inch or greater layer of shredded tree trimmings. Native cedar is the best choice.

Do not pile the mulch up on the trunk, do not build water dike rings, do not stake the tree except as a last resort, do not wrap the trunks under any circumstance, and do not thin out the top to compensate for root loss. These procedures are bad horticulture and a waste of money. They not only don't help the tree, they cause stress and increase the chance of problems and tree loss.

TREE PLANTING

Q. I just returned from South Carolina, where I was given a potted ginkgo tree to plant here. The friend who gave us the tree also indicated that female ginkgo fruit is rather foul smelling. My question is—how do you tell if a ginkgo is female?

A. The females are indeed the culprits. The fruit smells bad and is very messy. Unfortunately, there is no difference in the look of the two sexes, so you just have to keep your fingers crossed. Most of the trees in the nurseries claim to be males. The problem is—you won't know for sure for about fifteen years. My ginkgo was sold as a male fourteen years ago, and it is now producing fruit. The good news is the kernel inside the fruit is edible and has medicinal value.

Q. We have a beautiful, shady bois d'arc tree in our front yard. Is there any way that we can "start" new trees from it? I am a little concerned about the tree. I have noticed what appears to be mistletoe on one of the main branches.

A. It is not a highly recommended tree but can be grown easily from seed or cuttings. Cut the horse apples into quarters and let thoroughly dry before planting in potting soil. Cuttings are even easier. Small stem cuttings or large branches can be stuck in the ground, and they will almost always root. Farmers and ranchers have historically bent limbs of bois d'arc trees down to touch the soil, where they would root and form a living fence. You might want to take a look at my book *Plants of the Metroplex* to find more quality trees. Physical removal of the mistletoe is the only solution for that parasite.

Q. Last spring we were given twenty-two bare-root trees; twelve Shumard red oak, five lacebark elm, and five bald cypress. We planted them in 3-gallon buckets, and they have been growing well. Now we want to plant the trees. I know fall is the time to plant.

Question #1: Any special soil preparations required?

A. No—trees should be planted in the native soil of the designated site, although it is a good idea to improve the surface of the soil first by adding humate, lava sand, and compost.

Question #2: How often should they be watered during the fall/winter?

A. Depends on how much it rains. Don't overwater and don't let them dry out. Little additional water should be needed over the winter if the trees are planted properly.

Question #3: Should we prune before planting?

A. No, removing a percentage of the trees to compensate for root loss is very old-fashioned, outdated, and wrong advice—especially for container-grown trees that have all their roots in the container.

Question #4: There are cows grazing on our land. Should we take precautions to protect the trees?

A. Sounds like a fence is in order—usually a single-wire electric fence will work.

Q. I need some advice for planting acorns and nurturing them to grow here in the Waco area. I have as many acorns as would be needed to start a project for my two sons. Any help would be greatly appreciated.

A. Just plant the acorns as soon as they fall from the tree, in the soil or in pots with organic potting soil. The depth should be twice the length of the acorns. A more shallow depth should be used in controlled greenhouse conditions. Don't let the soil dry out, and watch out for the squirrels—they will be the biggest problem. If you use pots, leave them outside during the winter, but cover with mulch or floating row cover during severe freezing weather.

TREE PROBLEMS

Not only did lots of trees have strange foliage color one year, but many were dying. And it wasn't from old age. There was a heavier-than-usual advertising campaign that spring for "weed-and-feed" fertilizers. These are products that contain high-nitrogen, fast-acting synthetic fertilizers and toxic pre-emergent herbicides. Some of the products contain a synthetic herbicide, Atrazine, which the manufacturer admits kills shrub and tree roots. Trimec, a mixture of three other toxic herbicides, is in other weed-and-feed products. Warnings are stated on the bags. Since most residential properties have tree roots all over their entire sites, the damage from these products is widespread. The "weed-and-feeds," along with other synthetic herbicides, have many of our trees in serious trouble. Correct diagnosis is sometimes difficult because the damage to the trees doesn't always show up right away. When the foliage starts to turn funny colors, deform, and drop, the damage to the root system is often far advanced. The Sick Tree Treatment is part of the solution, but if you suspect or know that the Atrazine products were used, start by applying the activated-carbon product NORIT to tie up the toxins. Then drench the soil with Garrett Juice plus orange oil or d-limonene at 2 ounces per gallon. Products that contain molasses or dry molasses by itself will also help stimulate the microorganisms that break down the pollutants. You might also want to have a chat with the store that sold you this product—especially if your trees die.

TREE RECOMMENDATIONS

Q. I need to plant some trees. I like oak and pecan. I heard you talking about an oak tree that has big leaves, but I missed the name of the tree. You were also talking about native pecans having smaller but better-tasting pecans. Are all native pecan trees the same? Is there a specific name of native pecan I should buy? Where is the best place to buy trees? What should I do to prepare the ground for planting the trees?

A. Bur oak is the large-leafed tree I often mention. It is a fast-growing, long-living, relatively maintenance-free shade tree. It has very large acorns and so-so yellow fall color. Native pecans are now available from several garden centers. Specific selections that also have the small pecans are 'Kanza' and 'Caddo.'

TREE REPLACEMENT

Q. We lost a tree in the front yard last year. What type of tree would be the best to plant back? The area where we are going to replant this tree is about 12 yards in front of the house, and we were thinking about a pecan tree. Would there be any problem with this type of tree being planted that close to the house? If no problem, what type of pecan would be the best?

A. Several trees are planted less than 12 feet from my house, so I certainly hope that 12 yards is not too close. Pecan is an excellent choice, especially if you use a native or one of the small-nut hybrids such as 'Caddo' or 'Kanza.' Pecan is a good choice because in addition to being an excellent shade tree, the nuts are delicious and nutritious, especially when grown under an organic program. Some other good shade-tree choices to consider are Texas red oak, Texas ash, chinkapin oak, bur oak, Chinese pistachio, and cedar elm.

TREE ROOT/FOUNDATION PROBLEMS

Q. I've got a little problem here. As with most homes in the Metroplex, my slab foundation moves a little every summer. I recently hired a structural engineer to assess the situation, and he said I do not need any drastic measures—yet. He recommended a root barrier out in my back yard because I have two big trees out there sucking the moisture from the foundation. One is an ash and the other a silver maple. Both of these are beautiful trees, and I would estimate that the bases of both trees are in the 20-foot range from the slab. While the engineer did not know exactly where the root barrier should be placed, he suggested I contact a "tree person" before I dig the trench.

Before I call the proper authorities to mark where the underground cables are, I'd like to ask your advice on how far from the house/trees the root barrier should be, as well as how deep the trench should be. Also, do you have any suggestions as to what material I should use for the barrier? I know the root system of the silver maple is shallow, but what is the average depth of the ash root system?

A. I don't agree with the basic theory that trees growing around the house are a problem for the foundation, even if they are lousy trees like silver maple. Homes with trees growing near the foundation exist by the millions around the world, and foundation problems are not rampant. Drought and excessive rains combined with expanding clay soils are the most common culprits of slab problems. Well, that along with inferior-quality concrete work. Proper management of the landscaping is the solution. Soil that stays too wet should have its drainage improved, and soil that is too dry should be watered more carefully. The only way to keep tree roots away from the house is not to plant any trees on the property at all, which of course makes no sense. Tree roots only proliferate where conditions are good. The only way conditions could be good under a house foundation is if there is a water leak or severe drainage problems. Root barriers can be used, but they hurt the existing trees by killing off a large percentage of the root system. If you decide to install one, dig a ditch about 3 feet deep as far from the tree as possible and fill with coarse gravel. Do not use fabric barriers, especially those that contain herbicides. A better approach is to plant trees and shrubs where you want them for the best effect and maintain your place reasonably. Bottom line: Trees rarely cause foundation problems.

Q. **How close to the foundation of a house can a pecan tree be planted? I don't want the foundation to get in the way of the roots and stunt the growth of the tree.**

A. Folks are usually more concerned about the foundation than the tree. I like your attitude. Neither is a big concern, however. On normal residential sites, tree roots will eventually reach the house no matter how far from the structure they are planted. Some roots might go under the house, but most will hit the beam and travel laterally. That doesn't hurt the tree roots or the house if reasonable watering is done to prevent the soil from completely drying out. A more important issue is the danger of limbs or the entire tree falling on the house. That's why the most important question is the quality of the tree. I have trees growing so close to the house that the trunks are almost touching the eaves, but they are quality trees like Texas red oak, bur oak, live oak, Chinese pistachio, and cedar elm. Don't ever plant the fast-growing junk trees close to the house or anywhere on the site for that matter. Avoid Siberian elm, cottonwood, silver maple, fruitless mulberry, poplars, and willows. What's a reasonable distance to plant trees from the house? Around 20 feet on most sites. That's as good a number as any.

P.S. Pecans are fine, too. I have them as well.

TREE SEEDLINGS

Q. **My hometown of Irving is giving away tree seedlings next month, and each resident can have up to five. Choices are Arizona ash, live oak, cherry laurel, and sweetgum. Which would you say** are the better choices? I'm not sure what the size of these seed-lings will be, but would you advise me on how to care for a seed-ling to influence successful replanting? Should I plant outside now or when it gets bigger, give it a lot of water or not too much, and should I add anything to the soil to stimulate growth?

A. Live oak and sweetgum are the best of those choices. How-ever, sweetgum is not a good selection if white rock is near the surface. Open the packages as soon as you get the trees and plant them right away. Treat the roots with mycorrhizal fungi. Dig large, rough-sided holes, backfill with the native soil only, and settle the backfill with water instead of tamping. Cover the disturbed area with a mix of compost and lava sand followed by shredded native cedar mulch. No wrapping, staking, or thinning, please. Avoid the synthetic root stimulators, but it's okay to drench the roots with a seaweed or Garrett Juice solution.

TREES IN ROCKY SOIL

Q. What would be my best tree choices for rocky alkaline Hill Country soil with several feet of limestone beneath?

A. Large shade trees that will do the best in that condition are chinkapin oak, Texas red oak, Durand oak, Texas ash, and bur oak. Live oaks and cedar elms will also grow well in the black and white soils of Texas. The smaller-growing trees that favor that condition include Lacey oak, Bigelow oak, Mexican plum, rusty blackhaw vi-burnum, yaupon holly, and Eve's necklace.

Herbs

My definition of a herb is any plant that has a use other than just looking beautiful. My book *Herbs for Texas* covers them in detail, but here are some tips for you on some of my favorite plants

DISEASE-CONTROLLING HERBS

Herbs are easy to grow, they're beautiful, and they taste good, but we now have even more reason to use them. We've known for some time that cinnamon will at least repel and in some cases kill roaches and ants, but it and other herbs may do much more than that. Adding cinnamon to your food may help protect it and you against the deadly *E. coli* bacteria. And there's research to back it up. Food microbiologist Daniel Fung, at Kansas State University, has proven the power of cinnamon and four other common herbs that can kill the most dangerous strain of *E. coli* and other disease organisms. One of our favorite herbs, garlic, won the contest. The Kansas State Research study of twenty-three kitchen herbs and spices found that garlic killed the organism completely, but four others also killed the bacteria in various amounts. They included clove, cinnamon, oregano, and sage.

Researchers first tested twenty-three different herbs and spices against *E. coli* in the laboratory, then took the five that worked best and used them on store-bought ground beef that had been infected with 100,000 *E. coli* bacteria per gram. Again the bacteria died. Garlic and clove worked best. Garlic was the most effective in the laboratory study, and clove worked best when added directly to ground beef. All five killed *E. coli* to some degree. Another of Fung's studies combined the herbs with salami and other fermented sausages, and once again, the herbs controlled the pathogens on the food.

It has been reported that twenty thousand Americans are poisoned by *E. coli* annually and about 250 die. Whether that's accurate or not, this is exciting news about these nutritious herbs. Scientists at Oklahoma State University also discovered that horseradish and mustard can help fight *E. coli* and other food pathogens. Fall is the time to plant them. Even cinnamon and clove can be grown here if protected in the winter. Grow them in pots and move indoors when cold weather arrives.

EASY-TO-GROW HERBS

Q. We live in an area that is all rock but want to start a new herb garden. It has been recommended that we use sandy loam topsoil and then mix in compost. Do you agree? Also, should we add anything other than compost? And lastly, what herbs would you recommend for planting now and in the fall?

A. Spring is a great time to start many of the herbs. Annuals that can take the heat and produce well through fall include basil, lemon balm, lemon verbena, begonia, marigold, mint, perilla, purslane, stevia, and sweet Annie. Tropicals like aloe vera, scented geranium, and roselle can also be planted now in pots, to be moved indoors when the weather gets cold. Some of the wonderful perennials that can be started now include comfrey, elderberry, germander, hoja santa, oregano, purple coneflower, rose, rosemary, sage, southernwood, tansy, thyme, Turk's cap, wormwood, and yarrow. Herbal trees that can be planted now include ginkgo, jujube, linden, madrone, and witch hazel. In the fall, all the cool-season herbs can be planted. Try garlic (for sure), also alfalfa, arugula, chives, clover, coriander, dill, horseradish, parsley, and sorrel.

HERB TEA

Herb teas are good year-round, but as the weather cools these tasty and healthy drinks become more important. It's hard to beat steaming hot herb tea on a cold morning. There are plenty of herb plants that can survive cold weather; in fact, some are tough evergreens and can be left out all winter. Others are more delicate, will easily freeze, and therefore should be planted in pots so they can be moved to a protected area—house or greenhouse—when freezing temperatures are predicted.

Tea herbs that can be planted in the fall and left outdoors most winters—and here I'm talking about from Dallas south—include alfalfa, bay, calendula, dianthus, Johnny-jump-ups, lavender, some mints, oregano, pansies, rosemary, sage, and thyme.

The more delicate tea herbs can be planted in spring in pots and left outdoors during our wonderful fall weather. When freezes threaten, the potted plants can be brought indoors to a sunny window, a skylight location, or the greenhouse to give you a supply of tender herbs all winter for teas and other uses. This group includes anise hyssop, basil, dill, fennel, ginger, lemon balm, lemongrass, lemon verbena, sambac jasmine, and the tender mints. Cut foliage can also be frozen or dried and stored for use.

To prepare herb teas, I simply pick fresh leaves, seed, or appropriate flowers from herbs, put them in a ceramic teapot, and pour in hot water after bringing it to a boil. I use a glass kettle to boil the filtered water, and a ceramic teapot. It usually is not good to boil the leaves in the water because boiling destroys many of the healthy vitamins. In fact, letting the boiling water cool down slightly before pouring onto the herbs is a good idea. Let the brew steep from three to ten minutes, depending on your taste. Tannic acid increases with time and will make the tea bitter. A single herb or a mix of various plants can be used. I often use chocolate peppermint and lemongrass as a base and then add various other herbs to create different tastes. A good lemony tea, for example, is made from lemongrass, lemon verbena, and lemon balm. Japanese green tea also makes a good base.

To me, natural teas are great with nothing added, but lemon juice or honey can be added for taste. By the way, it really is important to use clean, filtered water. Chlorine and other contaminants can ruin the taste and quality of any good drink, as well as your health.

Unused tea can be poured on the plants as a liquid fertilizer after it has cooled. The other use is to drink it cold over ice the next day. Toss a couple of fresh leaves into your iced drink for additional flavor. The unused tea can also be frozen into ice cubes to be used in other drinks later.

Here's a more complete list of herbs and the parts to use for herb teas.

Alfalfa	Leaves and seeds
Angelica	Leaves, seeds, and roots
Anise hyssop	Leaves, flowers, and seeds
Basil	Leaves
Bay	Leaves
Blackberry	Leaves
Borage	Leaves and flowers
Burdock	Roots and seeds
Calendula	Flowers
Caraway	Seeds
Catnip	Leaves
Chamomile	Flowers
Chicory	Roots
Chrysanthemum	Flowers
Clover	Leaves and flowers
Coriander	Leaves, flowers, and seeds
Dandelion	Leaves and roots
Dill	Leaves
Echinacea	Roots, flowers, leaves, and seeds
Elecampane	Roots
Fennel	Leaves and seeds
Fenugreek	Leaves and seeds

Feverfew	Leaves and flowers
Flax	Seeds
Garlic	Cloves
Ginger	Roots
Ginkgo	Leaves
Ginseng	Roots
Goldenrod	Young leaves and flowers
Gotu kola	Leaves, stems, and roots
Hibiscus	Flowers
Hollyhock	Flowers (petals only)
Horehound	Leaves
Hyssop	Leaves, stems, and flowers
Lavender	Flowers
Lemon balm	Leaves
Lemon verbena	Leaves
Licorice	Roots
Linden	Flowers
Lovage	Roots
Marjoram	Leaves
Marsh mallow	Roots and leaves
Mint	Leaves and flowers
Monarda	Leaves and flowers
Mugwort	Leaves and flowers
Mullein	Leaves and flowers
Oregano	Leaves
Parsley	Leaves
Pepper	Fruit
Raspberry	Leaves
Rose	Petals and hips
Rosemary	Leaves and flowers
Sage	Leaves
Salad burnet	Leaves
Sambac jasmine	Flowers
Savory	Leaves
Saw palmetto	Berries
Scented geranium	Leaves
Strawberry	Leaves
Thyme	Leaves
Violet	Leaves and flowers
Yarrow	Flowers

Formula for Making Herb Tea

Q. When preparing herbal teas, do you normally use a regular or green tea as a base, and how much lemongrass/lemon balm/spearmint/etc. do you add? We made some the other day with chocolate spearmint, lemongrass, and lemon balm, but it was fairly weak and not too tasty. Just curious on the amount of ingredients to use. Enjoy your show and books.

A. Here's my formula for herb tea. Bring filtered water to a boil in a glass kettle. Put as many different fresh herbs as you can jam into a ceramic teapot. After the boiling water stops bubbling, pour over the herbs and let steep for 3–5 minutes. Add a little honey for taste and enjoy a delicious, healthy drink. Lemongrass is one of the herbs that needs to be bent and crushed to release the flavor. Lemon balm doesn't have much flavor. Try lemon verbena instead. I've never heard of chocolate spearmint—that may be the problem. There is a chocolate peppermint.

P.S. The best teapot in the world is the English Rockingham teapot from the Vermont Country Store catalog in Weston, Vermont (P.O. Box 3000, Manchester Center, Vermont 05255, 802-362-8440, web address: www.vermontcountrystore.com).

PEST CONTROL PROGRAM FOR HERBS

Add the following to Garrett Juice and spray as needed:

Garlic tea: Apply at ¼ cup/gallon or follow label directions for minor insect or disease infestations.

Citrus oil, orange oil, or d-limonene: Use at 1 ounce/gallon of water as a spray for insect pests, 2 ounces/gallon of water as a soil drench.

Potassium bicarbonate: 1 rounded tablespoon/gallon for fungal diseases.

Liquid biostimulants: Use per label.

Neem: Spray per label directions for serious insect and disease infestations.

Fish emulsion: Use at 2 ounces/gallon for additional nutrients.

Apply beneficial nematodes to the soil in early spring for thrips control. Do first spraying at bud swell just before flowering. First two sprayings should include Garrett Juice and garlic tea. Use additional sprayings as necessary. For best results, spray every two weeks, but at least once a month. When soil is healthy, nothing but Garrett Juice is needed in the spray.

BEGONIAS

Begonia semperflorens, or wax begonia, is an annual bedding plant that will sometimes perennialize during mild winters in the South. Planted in sun to part shade, begonias grow to a height of 6–15 inches, spread to 12–18 inches, and should be planted on a spacing of 9–12 inches. They are available with red, pink, or white summer flowers. The red leaf varieties can stand more sun; the green-leaf varieties need more shade. Propagation can be done by seed or cuttings. Begonias bloom non-stop throughout the summer if planted in loose, well-prepared beds, with lots of compost, rock minerals, and good drainage. Plant 4-inch pots in the spring, after the last freeze, for summer color in beds, hanging baskets, or pots. Potential problems include slugs, pillbugs, and cutworms, but these can be controlled with a dry mix of natural diatomaceous earth, hot pepper, and horticultural cedar. Plants grown in pots can be moved indoors and saved through the winter, although it is way too much trouble. Fertilize three times per growing season with organic fertilizer and spray every two weeks with Garrett Juice. Cut back leggy plants in summer for renewed blooming. Healthy plants will provide lots of delicious flowers for sherbet and other desserts, especially cold ones. The most overlooked asset of begonias is that the colorful blooms are delicious and can also be used in salads, desserts, and teas.

P.S. Don't eat the flowers of this or any other plant if you are still spraying toxic chemical pesticides.

ECHINACEA

Q. I have echinacea growing wild in my pasture and was wondering if you could tell me how and when to harvest it. Also, how do I tell the difference between *Echinacea purpurea* and other forms? My son won a cardamom plant in a local reading program, and we were also wondering how to harvest the cardamom.

A. Digging the roots during the winter is the best harvest time for *Echinacea*. All the purple coneflowers are similar in looks and apparently in medicinal quality. *Echinacea purpurea* may be a little darker purple. Some cultivars are white. I like them all. Cardamom seeds are collected and eaten or used to make tea when the plant matures. All other parts of the plant can also be used, but they have less medicinal value than the seeds.

HIBISCUS

A beautiful landscape plant that has additional uses is the wonder herb flowering hibiscus. Not only are these summer-color plants striking in beds or in pots, the flowers are edible and delicious. As with most large edible flowers, the reproductive parts should be avoided, as they can be bitter or even toxic in some cases. The petals, however, are wonderful in salads, as garnish, and even as a replacement for lettuce on sandwiches. I usually use the flower petals and lettuce. They not only taste good, they also add a strong splash of color to the food. Annual and perennial hibiscus will grow well here in North Texas. Here's more on these useful plants.

Perennial and tropical hibiscus should be planted in sun to part shade, but do best in full sun. They grow to a height of 5–6 feet and a spread of 3–6 feet. The final spacing should be about 2–3 feet. Hibiscus has single or double flowers in bright shades of pink, white, yellow, orange, purple, and many combinations. Annual hibiscus has smaller flowers, brighter colors, and shiny leaves. Those with huge, subtle-colored flowers and dull leaves are the perennial forms. Both can be propagated by cuttings or seed. The growth habit of perennials is upright on thick, succulent stems. The tropicals have more woody stems. Both bloom all summer and are easy to grow in any well-drained soil. They have moderate water and fertilizer requirements. Hibiscus are great for summer flower color and to use as specimens in pots or in beds—plus the flowers are edible. Minor problems include whiteflies, aphids, and leaf-chewing beetles. The tropicals, which act as annuals in most of Texas, are the most colorful. The hardy perennials will die to the ground in winter but return each spring. 'Frisbee,' 'Southern Belle,' 'Confederate,' and 'Marsh' are excellent perennial cultivars. *Hibiscus rosa-sinensis* is the Chinese or tropical hibiscus. *Hibiscus coccineus* is the perennial Texas star hibiscus. Fertilize hibiscus with cottonseed or fish meal once, and then add a small amount of Garrett Juice to the watering at least once a week. These plants bloom on new growth, so it's good to keep them well fed. Bat guano is also a good choice. These applications should be done in addition to the Basic Organic Program.

Q. I have a hibiscus bush in the back yard that has pink blooms. I also love hibiscus tea. How can I know if I can use the flowers from my bush to make tea? Are there varieties of hibiscus that are unsafe to eat (drink)?

A. The flowers of all hibiscus plants, both annuals and perennials, are edible and can be used in teas. Use only the petals, because the reproductive parts are bitter. The petals can be used in herb teas, in salads, as garnish, and with or instead of lettuce on sandwiches. There's only one precaution. Most wholesale growers still use synthetic fertilizers and toxic chemical pesticides to grow the plants you'll find in the garden centers. This is one of the main reasons to buy your plants from organic garden centers. At least the plants will have been maintained organically at the retail level. You can also use my detox program and use organic techniques for a while before eating any of the flowers. A month or so is normally a long enough time period. There are many other edible flowers—several are listed for you in my free handouts and on the web site www.dirtdoctor.com.

LEMON BALM

Q. I have been growing some lemon balm (*Melissa officinalis*) perennial herbs. They have developed brown outlines on the edges of the leaves. The plant looks very sick. What do I need to do?

A. Lemon balm is sometimes attacked by leafminers, especially when in stress from the heat of summer. The neem products work well to control the little beasts, but I would cut the plant back by at least 50 percent. Do it now, and the plant should put on new, fresh, insect-free foliage right away. By the way—one of my favorite summertime herb teas is a mix of lemon balm, lemongrass, and lemon verbena. Use a handful of the fresh leaves from each plant in a ceramic teapot. Add filtered hot water and enjoy hot or on ice. Honey and peppermint can be added for additional flavor.

OREGANO

Oregano, *Origanum* spp., is not only a perennial herb used for cooking, it is also an excellent ground cover for sun or partial shade, and it has few pest problems. Oregano grows to a height of 10–30 inches and spreads 18–30 inches and should be planted 12–18 inches apart. Flowers are white to mauvish purple in the summer. Propagation is done from cuttings, seed, and division. Greek oregano is my favorite and is easy to grow in well-drained garden soil, baskets, or containers. It is also winter hardy.

Oregano is used to flavor Greek and Italian food and is often called the pizza herb. It is used in tomato dishes and chili powders. Greek and Italian oregano are very similar, but Greek oregano is lower growing and the easiest to grow. Sweet marjoram is very similar. The unrelated plant Mexican oregano is primarily a decorative herb with tubelike lavender flowers. Cuban oregano is another striking ornamental plant that should be treated as an annual.

Oregano has several additional uses. It seems to deter insects with its strong odor. I use the foliage as a flavorful addition to my herb tea, and essential oil of oregano is used as a skin antiseptic.

PASSION FLOWER

Passion flower (*Passiflora* spp.) is a high-climbing perennial vine that grows in sun or light shade. Use 1- or 5-gallon plants at 3–6 feet on center. Few plants are needed because they tend to spread—aggressively in some cases. It has intricately detailed summer flowers in many colors, including whites, pinks, purples, and even reds, yellows, and oranges. Purple is the most common color. It can easily be propagated by cuttings. It climbs quickly by tendrils, has large, deeply cut leaves, and blooms almost all summer with spectacular flowers. It is easy to grow in any soil and fairly drought tolerant. Plants die to the ground each winter, but many species return in spring. The main problem is butterfly caterpillars—gulf fritillaries love this plant. Plant at least one plant just for the butterflies and handpick the larvae off the other plants. Some of the introduced varieties have the most dramatic flowers, but are not as winter hardy as the natives. There are four hundred species of passion flower, also known by the common names passion vine and maypop. The primary name comes from the flower parts that symbolize the crucifixion. The juicy oval fruit is used in drinks and ice cream and can be cooked into jellies and jams. The fruit grows to various sizes and colors and is reported to have aphrodisiac qualities and to calm nerves and headaches.

ROSES

Roses are the most misused of all plants. They are wonderful herbs. The petals are edible and excellent for teas and the fruit (hips) that follow the flower contain the highest concentration of vitamin C available. Using toxic chemical pesticides and fertilizers eliminates these uses—or it should! The typical rose chemicals are particularly bad because they are systemic, traveling throughout the plants and concentrating in the reproductive organs—the flowers and fruit.

Q. I am a beginner rose gardener. I planted my bushes in February this year and have been enjoying some blooming. I treat them with Miracle-Gro and have used the Bayer bug killer and rose feed on them. When a branch begins to bloom, I clip it to enjoy indoors. I am worried that I am harming my plants by doing too much clipping. Can you damage a rose by clipping all its blooms? I clip down about 10 inches from the bloom. It looks as if the angled cut is dried out on the bush. I have been doing this through mid-June. Five of the six bushes are still growing well, but one has not seemed to recover from my little trimmings.

A. The cuttings won't hurt the plant severely, but I am concerned about the products you are using. The fertilizer you used is synthetic and has no carbon, so I don't recommend it. The Bayer product is a toxic synthetic that of course I do not recommend. See below for my organic rose program.

Q. My roses are growing so tall that they have fallen almost to the ground. Also, I have noticed some brown spots on the leaves, maybe a fungus?

A. If your roses are climbing types, and it sounds as if they may be, pruning should wait until next spring after they have gone through their major bloom period. Pruning them now will severely reduce the amount of spring flowers. Bush roses, on the other hand, should be pruned in mid-February. The hybrids should be cut back about 50 percent; the antique roses should be only lightly pruned for shape. If you don't know whether your roses are old or one of the new fancy hybrids, prune lightly. There is some interesting research that indicates that meticulous rose pruning may not be worth the time.

To control the disease on the foliage, a comprehensive program is needed. Apply horticultural cornmeal to the soil at 20 pounds per 1,000 square feet and gently work into the soil. Mulch with shredded native cedar. The first spray with Garrett Juice plus potassium bicarbonate should be done just as the new growth starts to emerge in the spring. At the same time, beneficial nematodes should be added to the soil to control thrips.

Q. I have read your suggestions for organic rose care. I do not see any mention of pruning roses during our mild winter to stimulate new growth and maintain plant shape. I know your recommendations about pruning in general: "Don't prune." But I wondered about roses. I am a convert to the Natural Way and am now trying to convert all my neighbors. I wish I could convert the maintenance staff at Brookhaven Country Club. They are always using poisons and chemical fertilizers on the three golf courses here. Maybe one day they will get the message.

A. Since we finally got some cold weather, it is probably best to do the rose pruning now. Do as little pruning as possible, especially if your roses are antiques. Pruning is done more to maintain a more compact size, rather than to increase the health and flower production of roses. I haven't made much headway with golf courses yet, but Tierra Verde in Arlington is using some organic techniques, and they are trying to go 100 percent organic.

Organic Rose Program

Roses should only be grown organically, since they are one of the best medicinal and culinary herbs in the world. When they are loaded with toxic pesticides and other chemicals, that use is gone, or at least it should be. Drinking rose hip tea or using rose petals in teas or salads after spraying the plants with synthetic poisons is a really bad idea. For best results with roses, here's the organic program.

SELECTION

Buy and plant adapted roses such as antiques, David Austins, and well-proven hybrids. The old roses will have the largest and most vitamin C–filled hips. *Rosa rugosa* roses have the most vitamin C.

PLANTING

Prepare beds by mixing the following into existing soil to form a raised bed: 6 inches of compost, ½ inch of lava sand, ½ inch of decomposed granite, 30 pounds of wheat/corn/molasses soil amendment, and 20 pounds of sul-po-mag per 1,000 square feet. Soak the bare roots or root ball in water with 1 table-spoon of seaweed or Garrett Juice per gallon. Settle soil around plants with water—no tamping.

MULCHING

After planting, cover all the soil in the beds with 1 inch of compost or earthworm castings, followed by 2–3 inches of shredded native cedar. Do not pile the mulch up on the stems of the roses.

WATERING

If possible, save and use rainwater. If not, add 1 tablespoon of apple cider vinegar and 1 ounce of liquid humate per gallon of water. If all that fails, just use tap water but don't overwater. Avoid using salty well water.

FEEDING SCHEDULE

Round #1. February–March: organic fertilizer @ 20 pounds/ 1,000 square feet, lava sand at 80 pounds/1,000 square feet, and horticultural cornmeal at 10–20 pounds/1,000 square feet.

Round #2. June 1–15: organic fertilizer @ 20 pounds/1,000 square feet, Texas greensand @ 40 pounds/1,000 square feet or soft rock phosphate at 30 pounds/1,000 square feet if in acid-soil areas.

Round #3. September 15–30: organic fertilizer @ 20 pounds/ 1,000 square feet, sul-po-mag @ 20 pounds/1,000 square feet. Apply wheat/corn/molasses soil amendment at 30 pounds/1,000 square feet.

Foliar-feed with Garrett Juice twice monthly.

TURK'S CAP

Turk's cap, *Malvaviscus arboreus,* is a native Texan with red fezlike flowers in summer and red fruit that resembles rose hips. It is a deciduous perennial shrub and also a herb, because it has a use. It can grow in shade or filtered light and can be planted year-round. The flowers are excellent for attracting humming-birds and butterflies. You can dry the flowers and store them for year-round use. The red fruits are edible, but they are pulpy and mostly seed. A delicious herb tea can be made from the flowers or the fruit. The fruit can also be cooked down to produce a good jelly or syrup. This is one of the easiest-to-grow colorful perennials.

WITCH HAZEL

Q. I was wondering if witch hazel will grow here in our black clay soils. We do have spots of cotton root rot in our neighborhood. I was thinking of planting it in a bed near the house with an eastern exposure.

A. That's the perfect location for witch hazel. The reason I know? That is exactly where my tree is located. You probably already know this since you planted one, but for the other readers, witch hazel is a wonderful ornamental tree herb. The leaves can be used anytime, but for herb tea, the young leaves are best. Taken as tea, witch hazel is good for the skin, and it can be used as a gargle for sore throats. Extracts, lotions, and salves are made from the bark, stems, and leaves. You'll have to buy these as commercial products because they are made by distillation. This is a good-looking ornamental tree that should be used much more on residential and commercial projects.

Vegetables, Fruits, and Other Food Crops

Creating edible landscaping is one of my favorite parts of gardening. Planting designs don't have to just be pretty—they can be serviceable. Plants that function as trees, shrubs, ground covers, vines, perennials, and annuals can be used that provide food, culinary and medicinal herbs, insect control, dyes, and other benefits.

ALOE VERA

Aloe is an easy-to-grow tropical that is a must plant for every homeowner. It has to be protected in the winter, but it grows well indoors. It is also easy to propagate from the pups that grow up around the mother plants. The gel in the leaves is fantastic for treating skin problems, especially burns, and the flowers are edible.

BANANA TREES

Q. I planted four banana trees last year that multiplied like weeds. That is okay. Last winter we left them outside during winter. The stalks died back and came back in the spring. However, a wormlike bug settled in the leafy stalks and forced us to cut them back to ground and let them regrow. My question is how to care for them over the winter. Should I dig them up and place them in my garage, and if so, should I remove all leaves? Or should I cut them back to ground level before the winter?

A. Just after the first freeze, cut off the burned leaves and stalks slightly above the ground grade. Chop up the tops and toss into the compost pile or leave as mulch in the beds. Cover the stumps with a thick layer of shredded mulch. One additional step that would help with any insect problems in the future is to sprinkle orange or other citrus pulp around the stumps before covering with the mulch. As soon as the new foliage starts to emerge next year, spray the plant with Garrett Juice plus garlic tea. This is the first step of the organic pecan and fruit tree program. It works well for banana trees. Banana leaves can be chopped up and spread to repel fleas. Chickens also love the leaves. The fruit will mature in the most southern zones. Bananas are also planted as companion plants in orchards to help with insect control.

Q. **We have two groves of banana trees that began as two trees ten to twelve years ago. There are a dozen or more bunches of bananas this year, but we do not know when or how to harvest them. We cut one banana off carefully the other day, and it looked like a normal banana except the fruit was dry and a little like Styrofoam. Can you advise on when to harvest?**

A. The bananas are probably just not yet matured. They are tropical, of course, and need a long, warm growing season. It will be difficult for them in most parts of Texas. Even if they don't mature, enjoy the beauty of these big perennials.

COMPANION PLANTING

Q. **What kind of flowers help chase away bugs from vegetable gardens?**

A. The key to companion planting is to plant as many different kinds of flowering plants as possible. It also helps to have different color flowers that are blooming at different times throughout the season. The biodiversity helps to encourage a wide range of beneficial insects and hummingbirds, which help control pest insects and pollinate flowers. Use annuals and perennials, vines, shrubs, and trees that together provide a multitude of flower sizes, colors, fragrances, and times of bloom. Besides help with pest control, you'll have a beautiful garden.

HAIRY VETCH

Q. You said that planting hairy vetch was good for the soil and that tomato production really increased when planted where hairy vetch had been planted. We can't remember exactly what we are supposed to do when ready to plant tomatoes in the spring. Are we supposed to till the hairy vetch into the soil, then plant the tomatoes, or cut off the hairy vetch and plant the tomatoes into the root structure of the vetch?

A. When you are ready to plant the tomatoes, mow or hand trim the vetch off at the ground line and leave the clippings on the ground as mulch. Do not till. Plant the transplants right into the roots of vetch. Very little additional fertilizer is needed to literally double your tomato production for the year. Tomatoes can be set out early but only with protection of floating row cover or water walls. To be safe, wait until mid-April to set out transplants.

ONIONS

Q. My onions didn't do very well in the beginning. As my soil has gotten better, through compost, worms, and organic fertilizer, their size and juiciness has improved dramatically. That said, they are still very strong, and not sweet like the ones my father-in-law used to grow. My garden center recommended muriate of potash for all root crops, but my organic soil test in January 1999 showed my P&K (phosphorous and potassium) to be high already, so I am hesitant to add more potash. That test also showed my overall nitrogen high, but the available nitrogen was low and my pH was alkaline at 7.2. I added sulfur throughout last summer and sprayed my plants and ground periodically with fish emulsion, as was recommended. Is there anything you would recommend that might sweeten up my onions?

A. Muriate of potash is potassium chloride and very toxic to the soil and plant roots. It has been identified as one of the main causes of stress in fruit trees. It is not an acceptable fertilizer or soil amendment. Taste in food crops is primarily dependent on balanced soil containing the proper trace minerals such as copper, zinc, manganese, boron, molybdenum, and others. I don't recommend buying and applying these trace minerals separately because it is very easy to overuse them and cause toxic levels and new problems. These traces are available at the proper percentages and buffered in the basic organic products like compost, fish products, seaweed, earthworm castings, rock powders, and natural mulches. Foliar-feeding sprays, like the Garrett Juice formula that contains compost tea or humate, natural vinegar, liquid seaweed, and molasses, put the trace elements directly into the plants through the leaves and more quickly than they get through the roots. Sounds as if you are on the right track—the taste will get better every year, especially if the weather doesn't get hot early in the year.

Q. When onions start to seed, do you cut the seed heads off or let them go?

A. Remove the seed heads, but leave the foliage to continue to collect sunlight and manufacture sugars to build bigger bulbs. Breaking the tops over is a goofy old technique that does nothing but hurt the plant and the onion quality. Since onions have very small root systems, adding organic fertilizer directly under the bulbs will greatly help their size.

Q. We planted onions and potatoes around Valentine's Day, then later planted tomatoes and peppers. Everything was doing beautifully, and then our onions and potatoes started dying, as well as the tomatoes. The peppers are okay. We started looking at the sack of fertilizer we used, and it contained a weed killer. Is this what is causing our garden to die now?

A. Yes. You can see why I think those products should be off the market. Put down an activated carbon (NORIT or GroSafe) and then drench the soil with a mix of Garrett Juice and orange oil. The carbon will lock up the toxins, and the blend of other ingredients will do the detoxification. And, of course, don't use synthetic fertilizers ever again, especially the kind with toxic herbicides included. You might want to grow only ornamental plants in this area for at least a year. Adding zeolite at 40 pounds per 1,000 square feet and dry molasses at 10 pounds per 1,000 square feet will help speed up the decontamination.

PEPPERS

Even if you don't like the taste of peppers, you should consider planting some for other reasons. Sweet or mild peppers provide colorful fruit, and hot peppers are a source of one of the main ingredients for your homemade pest control. The sweet peppers that grow well here and provide good color include 'Golden Bell'—yellow, 'Valencia' or 'Araine'—orange, 'Pimento'—red, 'Lilac'—purple, and 'Top Banana'—yellow. Other good large red peppers include 'Big Bertha,' 'Emerald Giant,' and 'Jupiter.' Some of the hot peppers also have good color. Among the best are habanero—orange, Scotch bonnet—orange and red, cayenne—red, Spanish spice—yellow, purple Peruvian—purple, Serrano—red. Use a mix of the ripe, colorful fruit in baskets as gifts if you don't need all the peppers. Probably no one place will have all these varieties, so check around several places. One of the most disease-prone choices is a commonly sold pepper called 'California Wonder.'

Hot peppers are also great to eat if you like spicy food, but they have other uses as well. All the hot peppers can be dried by sun, an oven on very low heat, or a fruit drier. The dried pepper can then be ground into powder to serve as a pest control product. *Caution:* When grinding the extremely hot peppers such as habanero, wear a mask. The powder is extremely powerful and should not be breathed. My wife, Judy, can't even stay in the same room when I'm working with the high-octane peppers.

Hot pepper powder can be used alone or mixed with other materials. Pepper can be dusted on and around plants to ward off several pests. Most troublesome insects don't like the spicy application. Even slugs, snails, and pillbugs are repelled by hot pepper used as a fine powder or ground to the consistency of that used to flavor pizzas. For an even more powerful homemade product, mix equal parts hot ground pepper, natural diatomaceous earth, and horticultural cedar flakes. Sprinkle this mix around plants under attack. All three materials make effective soil amendments as well.

Pepper can also be used in liquid form. Garlic-pepper tea is one of my favorite mixes. It is made by adding the juice of two hot peppers together with the juice of two large garlic bulbs. Use the entire bulbs, not just individual cloves. I use a blender, some people like to cook the juice out of the fruit. Either way, add the juice of the four fruits to a gallon of water. That makes your garlic-pepper tea concentrate. Add ¼ cup of concentrate per gallon of spray. Add liquid seaweed at 1 ounce per gallon for even better control of spider mites and whiteflies, plus seaweed is an excellent foliage-feeding material. You can add the other Garrett Juice ingredients for the ultimate insect pest spray. Per gallon of spray, use 1 ounce of apple cider vinegar, 1 ounce of molasses, and 1 cup of compost tea, and the seaweed already mentioned.

Plant several pepper choices in the spring in well-prepared beds in sun or light shade. Yes, peppers will grow and produce quite well in shade. Probably the very best location is morning sun and afternoon shade, just as it is with many plants.

Bed preparation should include lots of compost, plenty of lava sand, and some Texas greensand and sugar. The best sugar is dry molasses, which should be used at about 5 pounds per 1,000 square feet. Use 3–6 inches of compost, 80 pounds or more of lava sand, and about 40 pounds of Texas greensand. Organic fertilizer should be used at 20 pounds per 1,000 square feet. Mulch the bare soil, after installing the transplants, with shredded tree trimmings—native cedar is the best. One final treat you can give the soil and the plants is to drench the soil with the Garrett Juice formula and spray the foliage at least monthly with the same or with fish emulsion and seaweed mix or whatever is your favorite organic spray.

Q. Every year we plant a number of hot peppers in our garden—jalapeños, cayenne, etc. Will the seeds from fruit that falls to the ground have an effect on onions or other plants planted the following spring? Also, could you provide the name and address of an organic soil-testing lab?

A. It would be highly unusual for the pepper seed to affect the other plants, though it might be interesting if they would. The only lab in Texas that gives accurate organic recommendations is Texas Plant and Soil Lab in Edinburg, Texas. The extraction system this company uses is very unique. It extracts the nutrients from the soil samples with carbon dioxide, which is just how plant roots do it. Other testing labs use harsh acids that break the soil down completely, which gives some interesting information about what the soil's ultimate makeup is, but these tests give no accurate information on what nutrients are available to the plants. Thus you receive no helpful information on how to fertilize or amend the soil efficiently and economically.

Q. I have been so pleased with the organic rose program and have had wonderful results. How is it possible to preserve (continue to grow inside or outside) a group of jalapeño plants that I grew from seeds last year? They are producing now, but winter is coming fast, and I would like to keep them growing.

A. Thanks for the rose report. Peppers in pots can be kept over the winter indoors if given plenty of light. Move them in before any freezing weather and be careful not to overwater. Your watering and fertilizing needs to be dramatically reduced during the dormant season. Peppers are perennial and can be kept for several years. They are also tropical and freeze easily. The only peppers that can be left outdoors as perennials are chili pequín and chili tepín.

Q. I planted some habanero pepper plants and so far have had good results. The problem I am having is the peppers are not changing colors. They are light green instead of orange, yellow, or red. Also, some of them are not hot; out of every five, a couple are very mild. What could cause this? I made some garlic-pepper tea about six months ago, and it smells even worse than normal. Can I still use it? How long is it good?

A. Habanero peppers are very slow to mature. You just have to be patient. Mine usually start turning orange in late summer. On the other hand, they are usable in the green form. They are extremely hot in any form. After handling these peppers, don't put your fingers near your eyes or on any tender skin. Why some of yours are mild is a mystery. Garlic-pepper tea can be kept for several months in the refrigerator, but the clumps of microbe growth (causing the odor) should be strained out with cheesecloth or old pantyhose. The power of the peppers may diminish over time, so as with most organic sprays, it's best to use them as soon as possible.

POTATOES

Q. I heard of a way to plant potatoes in a bushel basket with the bottom cut out. You put the potatoes on the ground inside of the bushel basket. As the plants grow, you cover them with mulch and leaves. When ready to harvest, just remove the basket, and you have potatoes with no digging. Think this will work?

A. Yes, that works well. A larger container would be better, just from a volume standpoint.

ROTATING CROPS

Q. You have mentioned that the forest doesn't rotate crops, so we shouldn't either. The forest adds compost daily through animal feces, dead animals, and leaves. In a garden, we take and take and take from the soil. Bringing in compost from other areas robs from one area of the earth to build up another. I'm not saying that is wrong, it's just the way it is. For people who can't or don't add back to the soil (like you mentioned they should do), resting the soil is probably a good idea. It came from the Old Testament when God told the people to rest the land every seven years. That gave the soil a chance to rebuild. Doesn't rotating crops help fight pests? Or does it just make the pests move all over the garden instead of just staying by the plants they like to eat?

A. You're right except for one point. During the fallow period, where does the additional rock powder and organic material come from? I admit that when we are growing food crops, we are force-growing ill-adapted plants in most cases and need to replenish the soil after each crop. The fallow year may temporarily eliminate food sources for insect pests and microbe pathogens, but without volcanic eruption or flood, I'm not sure how the remineralization will happen. Rotating crops is okay to do but probably not essential. Dr. William Albrecht, the father of soil science at the University of Missouri, wrote years ago that it is the quickest way to mine the minerals from the soil. Not only do forests not rotate crops, neither do grasslands or any perennial plant stands.

SWEET POTATOES

Q. What is the best way to grow sweet potatoes? What is the best way to store them?

A. They are started as slips in the greenhouse in the winter and then set out after the air and soil are warm in the late spring. Grow them in healthy soil in full sun. Sweet potatoes should be stored after harvest in the summer in a cool, dry place and eaten as soon as possible.

TOMATOES

Q. I am having major problems with my tomatoes. A majority of them are stunted, with their leaves curled and knotted. I planted them in a raised bed with great soil that has plenty of compost, lava sand, greensand, and worms in it. I figured it would be a great place for my tomatoes. Can you tell me what is wrong with the tomatoes and can I help them? I have been spraying once a week with Garrett Juice.

A. May be a virus—very tough to control. Try drenching the soil with one of the neem products. It is one of the few pest control products that does seem to have an effect on viral diseases. The other possibility is herbicide damage. Unfortunately, there are lots of herbicides in the air, such as Roundup, 2,4-D, Manage, Oust, Picloram, Clopyralid, and others. If that's the case, treat the soil with NORIT activated carbon (GroSafe), apply the wheat bran/cornmeal/molasses dry mixture, and then drench the area with Garrett Juice plus d-limonene or orange oil at 2 ounces per gallon.

Q. I live in an apartment with western sun on my deck, and this is my first year with a total organic program. My problem is my tomato plants. I have four different types in individual 5-gallon plastic pots, and they are over 5 feet tall. I water them with about ½ gallon of water every three days. I have a lot of buds that never bloom and look almost fried. Now all the leaves are dying, but the vines still seem healthy. What am I doing wrong?

A. Container plants must be watered every day in most cases, especially when the temperatures are over 90 degrees. On the other hand, you need to be careful that the drainage in the pots is good and the roots aren't staying too wet.

VEGGIE WASHES

Q. I would like to know if you have a recipe for a fruit and vegetable wash to remove dirt and pesticide residue and wax that is on our vegetables and fruit. There is one on the market that says it uses 100 percent natural sources. Well, there must be a recipe that one could make at home, one would think. I would appreciate any information or advice you may give me. Thank you.

A. There are several commercial products, but if you make your own, add 1 ounce of orange oil or d-limonene to 1 quart of water. Some people also use hydrogen peroxide straight from the drugstore or grocery store.

Wildflowers
and Wild Flowers

There are wildflowers and there are wild flowers. Plants that I call "wild flowers" are one of our greatest natural resources. It's not just the low-growing annuals and perennials that provide pleasing color. Flowers, colorful foliage, and berries flaunt colorful displays in many forms, including vines, shrubs, and even trees. All these wild flowers are effective in residential and commercial landscapes as well as along roadsides.

Taking advantage of color from wild native plants has many benefits. With careful selection of plant materials, gardeners and landscapers can have spring and summer flowers, fall foliage color, and striking winter berries and seedpods. These plants are reasonably priced, easier to maintain, and longer lasting than the cultivated exotic annuals and short-lived perennials that have become too much the norm in the nursery and landscape industry. Natives are the best choices for organic management programs. Non-native wildflowers have become somewhat popular, but hopefully that misstep will soon fade away. These poorly adapted introductions are sometimes showy the first spring, but they don't last well and don't return for more color each year, as the natives do. Using them is simply a bad investment, not to mention bad horticulture. They are a strange-looking, out-of-place, cosmetic blemish. Come to think of it, their short life is a good point.

One of the new techniques we have discovered is a change in the timing of wildflower seed planting. Rather than planting the spring-blooming flowers in the fall, better establishment and color result from planting them in the summer. Why? That's when Mother Nature does it. It's the natural thing to do. It probably has to do with sunlight, heat, and soil microbes. Another rare recommendation is to buy and use unscarified seed. It isn't natural for all the seed to germinate at once. Scarification can result in crop loss. Better long-term results come from allowing seeds to germinate over a period of years. Another recommended planting change relates to the wild flowers. When planting trees, shrubs, vines, and other woody permanent plants, dig a wide, rough-sided, saucer-shaped hole. Set the plant so that the top of the ball is slightly above the ground grade, and backfill with nothing but the soil from the hole. Water thoroughly and let the weight of the water settle the soil—no tamping, in other words. Mulch the disturbed area with shredded native tree trimmings. Native cedar (*Juniperus* spp.) is the best mulch choice. Do not wrap the trunks, stake, or prune to thin out these plants. Very few losses will occur if you follow this cost-effective program.

One of the most powerful changes we can make to the management of roadsides, parks, and other natural areas is to work with Mother Nature rather than try to control her. It can't be done, so why try? The most impressive roadsides in Texas occur where smart management has been applied. It is no accident that in districts where herbicides have been avoided, native grasses, wildflowers, and wild flowers have flourished. More and more people are learning that native plants work well along highways, in parks and on golf courses, in the home garden, and in commercial landscaping. Maintenance costs and water availability become bigger issues every year for all of us. The thoughtful use of these drought-tolerant wild flower plants can go a long way toward relieving the problem.

Wild flowers, available in the forms of annuals, perennials, shrubs, vines, and trees, have wonderful flower displays and in many ways are much easier to grow and more dependable year after year. Not that bluebonnets, Indian paintbrush, and evening primroses aren't impressive, it's just that we have many more choices. As shown in the tables below, landscaping that is beautiful, colorful, not overly hungry or thirsty, and easy to maintain can be done with many different kinds of native Texas plants.

WILD FLOWER SHRUBBY PLANTS

Common Name	Botanical Name	Color/Special Features
Agarita	*Berberis trifoliolata*	Red fruit in summer
Cactus	Many species	Yellow or red flowers; purple prickly pear even has purple pads
Turk's cap	*Malvaviscus arboreus*	Red flowers in summer followed by red fruit
Yucca	*Hesperaloe parviflora*	Red flowers in summer
Yucca	*Yucca* spp.	White flowers in spring

WILD FLOWER TREES

Common Name	Botanical Name	Color/Special Features
Black cherry	*Prunus serotina*	White spring flowers
Desert willow	*Chilopsis linearis*	Light pink to violet or white orchid-like summer flowers
Eve's necklace	*Sophora affinis*	Wisteria-like pink flowers in spring
Flowering dogwood	*Cornus florida*	Pure white, pink, or rose flowers in spring
Fragrant ash	*Fraxinus cuspidata*	Fragrant white spring flowers

Common Name	Botanical Name	Color/Special Features
Madrone	Arbutus xalapenis	Creamy white to pale pink flowers in the spring; raspberry-like fruit in the fall
Mexican buckeye	Ungnadia speciosa	Clusters of lavender spring flowers
Mexican plum	Prunus mexicana	Fragrant, small white spring flowers
Native hawthorn	Crataegus spp.	Small white spring flowers
Redbud	Cercis canadensis	White or lavender spring flowers
Rough-leaf dogwood	Cornus drummondii	White flower clusters and white fruit
Rusty blackhaw viburnum	Viburnum rufidulum	White spring flowers, red fall color
Scarlet buckeye	Aesculus pavia var. pavia	Red spring flowers
Texas mountain laurel	Sophora secundiflora	Fragrant, violet wisteria-like flowers in spring

WILD FLOWER VINES

Common Name	Botanical Name	Color/Special Features
Clematis	Clematis texensis	Red or purple flowers in the spring; distinctive lantern-like flowers
Coral honeysuckle	Lonicera sempervirens	Thin red flowers in the summer are excellent for attracting hummingbirds.
Crossvine	Bignonia capreolata	Yellow and/or red trumpet-shaped flowers in spring
Wild roses	Rosa spp.	Fragrant, various colors, edible hips

COMMON WILDFLOWERS

Here are the plants typically considered wildflowers.

Common Name	Botanical Name	Color	Special Features
American basketflower	Centaurea americana	Lavender spring blooms	Good for attracting butterflies, dove, and quail
Bluebonnet	Lupinus texensis	Blue and white, early spring	Poisonous to horses
Butterfly weed	Asclepias tuberosa	Orange in summer	Primary host plant for Monarch butterflies
Clover, crimson	Trifolium incarnatum	Dark red spring flowers	Flowers are delicious in salads. Leaves of all clovers must be cooked before eating to prevent bloating.

Common Name	Botanical Name	Color	Special Features
Clover, white	*Trifolium repens*	White summer flowers	Herb tea is made from the flowers.
Columbine	*Aquilegia canadensis*	Small red-and-yellow summer flowers	Will even grow in solid rock.
Coreopsis	*Coreopsis tinctoria*	Red and yellow	Flowers provide a yellow dye for use on wool. Plants are used to repel insect pests.
Engelmann daisy	*Engelmannia (pinnatifida)* now called *peristenia*	Yellow summer flowers	Has been used as an excellent forage for livestock.
Evening primrose	*Oenothera* spp.	Pink spring flowers	Can be invasive but quite showy in late spring. Attracts beneficial ground beetles.
Gayfeather	*Liatris* spp.	Dramatic purple spikes	Wonderful cut flower; color lasts well in arrangements. Harvest sparingly and take care not to hurt the crown of the plant.

Common Name	Botanical Name	Color	Special Features
Horsemint	*Monarda citriodora*	Lavender spikes	Fresh or dried flowers and leaves can be used as an insect repellent. Too strong for tea use.
Indian blanket	*Gaillardia pulchella*	Red-and-yellow flowers in late spring	Legend has it that an old blanket maker was honored by the Great Spirit by replicating his burial blanket with this beautiful flower.
Indian paintbrush	*Castilleja indivisa*	Red-orange spring flowers	Biological activity and even the roots of other nearby flowers are important for the growth of paintbrush.
Indian paintbrush	*Castilleja purpurea*	Reddish-orange, yellow, or purple spring flowers	Perennial form of Indian paintbrush
Maximilian sunflower	*Helianthus maximiliani*	Yellow summer flowers	Perennial sunflower with edible roots, similar to but smaller than Jerusalem artichoke

Common Name	Botanical Name	Color	Special Features
Mexican hat	*Ratibida columnifera*	Red and yellow flowers with drooping petals	Tough perennial that often doesn't bloom until the second season
Purple coneflower	*Echinacea* spp.	Purple summer flowers	All species of *Echinacea* have immune-enhancing properties.
Snow-on-the-mountain	*Euphorbia marginata*	White-edged leaves and summer flowers	Good for cut flower use. Stem is irritating to some people.
Tahoka daisy	*Machaeranthera tanacetifolia*	Lavender daisylike blooms primarily in summer	Long-lasting bloom period
Verbena	*Verbena* spp.	Purple summer flowers	Several varieties are available.
White yarrow	*Achillea millefolium*	White summer flowers	Good roadside wildflower and excellent contrast for other flower colors
Winecup	*Callirhoe involucrata*	Late spring, wine red flowers	Easy-to-grow perennial

And don't forget the native grasses. They offer graceful foliage through the summer and decorative seed head displays in fall and winter. Those that should be used more in the landscape include sideoats grama, Eastern gammagrass, switchgrass, Indiangrass, big and little bluestem, blue grama, inland seaoats, Lindheimer's muhly, Texas bluegrass, and buffalograss.

BLUEBONNETS

Q. What is the process called in which bluebonnet seeds are scratched or scored to enable them to break through the seed covering in a shorter time? Also, when is the best time to sow bluebonnets? I have tried with the little plants but have never been successful in having them seed themselves. I have a virtual sea of Indian paintbrush and would love to have bluebonnets among them.

A. The term is scarification, but I don't recommend it for bluebonnets. The timing of your question is good. When we see the bluebonnets in bloom, we should think about getting ready to plant more. Most horticulturists would tell you to wait till next fall to plant the seed. That's not the best advice. When does Mother Nature plant the seed? When the flowers dry and the seedpods shatter—late spring right? The seed may need the heat of summer, the microbes that like summer, the ultraviolet rays, or something else. Don't scarify the seed, broadcast them in the summer, and you might see some impressive results.

Turf

What's the best grass, what's the best soil preparation, what's the best turf maintenance program? These are some of the most common questions I get every year.

Turf grass choices for North Texas include St. Augustine, common Bermuda, hybrid Bermudas, zoysia, centipede, and buffalo. The best turf is a mixture of several grasses and forbs, but if you must choose just one, here's a rundown.

CHOOSING WHICH GRASS TO PLANT

Bermudagrass is planted by seed as well as by solid sod. It is best in full sun and requires less water and fertilizer than St. Augustinegrass. Its flaw is its aggressiveness; it spreads fast. That's good when trying to get it to grow and complete the turf, but it's bad when it spreads into the beds—which it commonly does. It can become a horrible weed. Bermudagrass is durable to traffic.

The hybrid Bermudas are finer-textured selections of the parent grass. They are sterile (produce no viable seed) and require more intense maintenance because flaws and weeds show up so much. These grasses are primarily used on golf courses and home putting greens.

Buffalograss is my favorite grass. It is our only native turf grass and must be grown in full sun. It has extremely low water and fertilizer requirements and no pest problems. Winter cold and summer heat stress just don't bother this grass. The critics who love the high-nitrogen fertilizers and pesticides complain that Bermuda invades buffalograss and takes it over, making it a bad choice. Well, Bermuda will take over buffalo if too much watering and fertilizing is done. The native buffalograss is planted from unhulled seed and takes about two full growing seasons to be thick. Hulled seed is also available, and it will establish much more quickly. The hybrids are the best choices if budget allows. They include 'Prairie,' '609,' and 'Stampede.' 'Stampede' is the only one to receive less than glowing reports. They should all be planted as solid sod.

Centipede is similar to St. Augustine in appearance and needs, but it's for those of you with sandy soil. It can be grown in partially shaded areas to full-sun areas and is relatively maintenance free. It can also be blended with St. Augustine, clover, dichondra, violets, and other good lawn forbs.

St. Augustinegrass is the best choice for shady areas, but even it needs about a half day of full sunlight to thrive. It also has problems with a fungus called brown patch, or *Rhizoctonia*, when fertilized and watered too much. The organic program is a preventive measure, and the use of cornmeal on problem spots is an effective cure. St. Augustine should be planted as solid sod. Spot-sodding costs about as much and gives a spotty, bumpy, weedy effect for several years. No hardy seed is available at this time. It is the most susceptible of these grasses to freeze and drought damage.

Zoysiagrass is a beautiful, lush grass that is touted as the king of grasses and the most durable of them all. Nothing could be further from the truth. Zoysia is the slowest-growing grass. As a result, it is easily worn out from traffic—mailperson's path, kid's play, dogs, and so on. It heals so slowly that weeds and other grasses can easily get started. This grass should only be used for viewing areas. If the turf is to have any wear and tear from any kind of traffic, plant something else. If zoysia does fit your low-use program, plant by solid sod only. Don't ever buy the mail-order plugs. You should always buy any grass from local suppliers.

The seedbed preparation for turf grasses is simple. All these plants like the same amendments—organic matter and rock minerals—although they will all respond well to compost, humate, organic fertilizers, lava sand, and Texas greensand. Bermuda and buffalo need very little of these amendments for establishment. Use 5–20 pounds of each amendment per 1,000 square feet for best results. The rates are not critical. That's one of the nice features of the organic technique. When you plant solid sod of any kind, fill in the cracks between the solid-sod pieces with compost. Don't scalp anytime, mow at whatever height you like, and use the Basic Organic Program to maintain your turf with a minimum amount of trouble.

BERMUDAGRASS SEED AND CORNMEAL

Q. Can I broadcast Bermudagrass seed with cornmeal with any good results? If not, what else?

A. Cornmeal shouldn't hurt germination of the seed, but it does contain about 10 percent corn gluten meal. Just make sure it's plain or horticultural cornmeal and not the natural pre-emergent, which is pure gluten. Corn gluten meal is quite effective preventing small seed from establishing. To be completely sure, don't use the cornmeal.

BUFFALOGRASS

Q. We have sodded buffalograss. It is full of dallisgrass. As we pull the weeds out, they leave big holes in the sod. Should they be filled in, and if so, with what? Our dirt is red sand from the building pad, then the black hard clay the sod came in from South Texas. Some have advised putting sand over the top. Any suggestions?

A. Fill the voids with a mix of compost, Texas greensand, and lava sand. Use a third of each. The grass will fill into these areas quickly. A light topdressing of the same mix would be helpful.

Q. I am convinced buffalograss is the way to go for a lawn at a newly built house. However, I am told that buffalo is not at all durable for traffic (dogs, kids, etc.). Any truth to this? Is it not a good

choice for high-use areas? Also, the Texas Veterans Land Board Green Building Program gives high points for using buffalograss as your lawn in new homes. This can help reduce interest rates substantially.

A. Well, that's some pretty cool information about the interest rates, but the advice you received on buffalograss is 180 degrees off base. Buffalo is our only native turf grass, and it is the most drought-tolerant and wear-resistant choice available. It makes Bermuda and St. Augustine look like real weenies in the summertime. It will not grow well in the shade. Zoysia is the least wear resistant of all summer grasses.

FESCUE

Q. I have planted tall fescue grass the last two years in the fall. It starts out beautiful in the spring, then, despite how much I water, it dies. I planted it over old Bermudagrass that was almost dead. Since the fescue grass is dead now, the Bermuda is still sick looking. Do I need to start completely over, or is it possible to replant and doctor the sod?

A. Fescue usually needs to be replanted each year and especially after the extreme summer temperatures and drought. The timing is the same for perennial rye, clover, vetch, and other cool-season grasses and legumes. The ideal date is usually around September 15. Perennial rye is less permanent and a better choice than annual rye if you want to continue to grow the Bermuda in the summer.

FUNGAL TURF DISEASES

Some fungal diseases start to show up with the cooler weather, especially if you are still fertilizing with synthetic, high-nitrogen products. The cure for fungal diseases in the short term is to apply horticultural cornmeal at 10–20 pounds per 1,000 square feet. This technique works well for brown patch in St. Augustine and other grass pathogens such as fading out, gray leaf spot, rust, *Pythium* blight, and slime mold.

Cornmeal will also control fairy rings and other mushrooms and toadstools.

GRASS AND TREE ROOTS

Q. I am planning to replant grass under my mature American elm. I also want to improve the soil. What precautions should I take to protect the tree, but not doom the grass at the same time?

A. Add a thin layer of compost (about ¼ inch) and 20 pounds each of compost, lava sand, Texas greensand, and horticultural cornmeal per 1,000 square feet. Don't till—that destroys the beneficial fungi and feeder roots. Fill in the cracks between the sod blocks with compost or earthworm castings. Since the shade is heavy under American elms, you might want to use a ground cover instead of grass, especially if you are thinking about planting grass seed. Choices include English ivy, ophiopogon, liriope, or the natives—horseherb, frog fruit, and snakeroot.

GRASSBURS

Q. I am looking for a surefire and quick way to rid myself of the stickers and get some grass growing, short of spending lots of money on pallets of St. Augustine sod.

A. Grassburs are present on your site for one reason and one reason only—you have sandy, infertile soil. Improve the health of the soil, and the grassburs and other pioneer plants will vanish. Add organic matter. If humus and humic acid are present in the soil, grassbur seed will not germinate. To speed up the availability of humic acid and the resulting weed control, broadcast corn gluten meal at 20 pounds per 1,000 square feet. The timing is March 1. Leonardite and other humate products will also help, and they can be applied anytime. Apply them at 10 pounds per 1,000 square feet.

Q. I have nearly an acre of sand. I can reach down and pull up turf just as if I was digging on the beach. We just bought this place in June. The yard is full of grassburs. I'm being told to put down a pre-emergent—Betasan. What's the Natural Way?

A. Toxic chemicals aren't good to use anytime, but fall is the treatment time for winter grasses and weeds, not for summer annuals like grassburs. The overall Basic Organic Program is the best control for grassburs and other seasonal weeds. You can apply humate and dry molasses now for general soil improvement, but the specific treatment is corn gluten meal at 15–20 pounds per 1,000 square feet. The timing for application should be about March 1.

GRASS CLIPPINGS

Q. Since I do not pick up grass clippings, I don't have a lot of green material to add to my compost pile. Most of my neighbors, who don't do organics, do catch their clippings and put them at the curb for pickup. Since the clippings probably have chemical fertilizer and pesticides on them, is it okay to use those in my compost pile or not?

A. These people are not only wasting your and my tax money and jamming up the landfills, they are throwing away valuable natural resources. Yes, the clippings—from folks silly enough to put them in plastic bags on the curb, destined for the dump—are most likely contaminated with toxic chemicals. However, the best way to detox those materials and make them useful is to compost them. The microbial activity in the pile will disassemble the compounds and render them usable. There is one exception: if they have used any of the SU (sulfonylurea) herbicides or a specific product called Clopyralid, they should not be added to your compost.

GRASS REMOVAL

Q. What is the earliest date that we can spray to kill the grass and till the soil to begin a project of planting nandina, grass, and Asian jasmine?

A. I recommend you physically remove the grass, prepare the beds, and install all the permanent plants, including grass sod, as soon as possible. This can be done in any season. The grass can be scraped away or removed with a sod cutter. Landscape companies offer this service. Of course, I never use the toxic herbicides like

Roundup, but even the organic choices like vinegar and orange oil won't be effective except in the summer when the grass is green. Complete establishment of the plants will be much faster than if you wait to start in the late spring. If that is not the decision, and spraying to kill the grass is the plan, use 10 percent (pickling) vinegar full strength with 2 ounces of orange oil (d-limonene) and add 1 teaspoon of liquid soap per gallon of spray. You will have to wait to apply this spray until the weather and soil are warm enough for the grass to be actively growing.

LAWN LEVELING

Q. My lawn has some low areas. What is the best product to level it? What is the best time of year to do this?

A. Hire a landscape company to core-aerate the lawn and then rake the removed soil cores down into the low areas. This cutting and filling is the best and most natural technique. The second best approach would be to buy and spread topsoil that is as close to the native soil as possible. The third choice would be to bring in a mix of good organic amendments such as a one-third-each mixture of lava sand, Texas greensand, and compost. The worst choice is to bring in washed concrete sand or any soil that is different from the existing kind. Any soil applied to the surface more than ½ inch will smother the grass and damage tree roots in the area.

RYEGRASS AND OTHER COVER CROPS

If you have decided to overseed your summer grasses with ryegrass, late summer is the time. Scalp the Bermuda or St. Augustine and aerate the soil for even better results. Broadcast perennial ryegrass at 7–10 pounds per 1,000 square feet. Annual rye is cheaper but coarser, and harder to get rid of in the spring. Water daily until the grass is established, and then cut back to a regular schedule, which will vary depending on sun or shade, soil type, drainage, and other factors.

When planting any legumes such as clover and vetch, it's best to inoculate the seed with the proper rhizobial bacteria.

The garden centers and feed stores can tell you which to buy. They also usually have good instructions on the packages as well. The inoculation is no longer needed after being organic for a while and healthy soil has been created. The bacteria will naturally exist in the soil.

Q. I have claylike soil. I had overseeded with perennial rye the last weekend of September. Around mid-October, after the rye had come up, I broadcast corn gluten meal. Then toward the end of October, I decided I wasn't satisfied with the rye coverage. I didn't know if any new seed would germinate, since I had spread corn gluten meal. You said to go ahead and put out some more seed and try to keep the ground moist, as it would slow the corn gluten meal's pre-emergent properties. Well, I did as you advised, and it worked very well. I now have nice, even coverage with my rye, and the yard looks great!

Now, on to my question. I would like to give the buffalograss a try and see how it does with my Bermuda. I'm in a similar situation as above, though, because I still would like to apply more corn gluten meal this spring. How do you recommend I coordinate the two? I'm thinking corn gluten meal early and seed later, but I wanted to check with you first.

A. Thanks for the report. On the buffalograss, it would probably be best not to mix the corn gluten meal and the grass. Buffalo doesn't need high fertility. The corn gluten meal provides high fertility and pre-emergent qualities. You'd better do the weeding in the buffalograss by hand. One of the great advantages of this grass is its low fertility requirement.

SOD

Q. I have seen your article on summer grasses, and you do not recommend planting sod after August 1. The article mainly talked about Bermuda and buffalograss. Does this same rule apply to St. Augustine? If it does not, how late in the fall can St. Augustine be planted as sod?

A. The article was about planting from seed. Solid sod can be planted year-round when available, especially if we continue to have mild winters. No one would argue that there's no risk. If we have another severe 1983–1984-type winter, newly planted grass of any kind will be lost—as would the established turf grasses.

SPRING WEEDS, GRASS PLANTING

The overwhelming winner of the most questions lately is weeds. The questions and comments have ranged all over the map. Some gardeners report the most beautiful lawns in the neighborhood and attribute them totally to the organic program. Others, mostly organic beginners, have complained that their lawn is the worst on the block—mostly weeds—and that the lawns maintained by the green-and-white trucks look better.

Some common denominators emerge. First of all, the value of overseeding in the fall with ryegrass shows up strongly now. Those who didn't overseed are suffering the weed-spotted lawns. The ryegrass lawns look gorgeous. The rye crowds out most of the weeds, and those few that exist blend in visually. Check around town in the spring—you can easily see what I mean. Mark your calendar now to overseed in late summer with perennial rye. The seed costs a little bit, and a few more mowings are needed, but the spring weed problem will basically be eliminated.

Now—if you didn't overseed, you probably do see more weeds than normal. One reason is the mild winter. Cool-season weeds have been germinating and flourishing all winter. Henbit is the easiest to eliminate—just mow it. Annual bluegrass (*Poa annua*), dandelions, chickweed, and others can be mechanically removed with tools such as the Weeder or the Weed Popper, or they can be sprayed with full-strength vinegar. Ten percent pickling vinegar is available in the grocery stores, and 20 percent is available in the garden centers and feed stores that sell organic products. If you add 2 ounces of molasses per gallon of spray or 2 ounces of orange oil, the spray works even better. This is a nonselective herbicide and will burn or kill the good plants as well as the weeds, so spray carefully. For those who don't like to mix home brews, commercial products—including Garden-Ville Organic Weed Control, Burn Out, and Weed Eraser—are in the stores. All these products work best on sunny, warm days.

My favorite way to handle weeds is to mow them. They are green and present for a reason. Mother Nature sends in the weeds to cover bare soil and to help build unhealthy soil. As you improve the health of the soil with organic fertilizers, compost, volcanic rock, and sugars, the need for the weeds goes away and so do the weeds. You might still have time to get some control of summer weeds like crabgrass and grassburs by applying one of the humates and some corn gluten meal. Weeds in beds? Cover them with mulch. Shredded native cedar is the best. A little hand pulling is appropriate, too.

Do not scalp lawns in the spring unless you need to plant new grass. In that case, scalp first, then rototill 1 inch into the ground. That kills the crowns of the weeds but leaves the roots in place to rot, which will help to aerate and build the soil. Plant the new seed or sod and water till the turf is established. The only bed prep needed for new grass planting is a light application of compost or humate and some lava sand. Amounts aren't critical. If you plant solid sod, fill in the cracks between the blocks with a finished compost.

Oh, and one more point—don't ever catch the grass clippings. You'll improve the soil, save time, and actually enjoy mowing the lawn if you leave the clippings on the turf.

Q. I sodded part of my back yard with St. Augustine last year, and ever since I continue to get bunches of mushrooms growing up just after it rains. Since I have little kids who try to eat everything, I would like your suggestions on how to get rid of them. I tried cornmeal, but my dog ate the mushrooms then.

A. Lots of old organic matter decaying in that soil is the cause. Couple of things you might try—sulfur at the recommended level of 5 pounds per 1,000 square feet or spray with baking soda at 1 rounded tablespoon per gallon of water. Mushrooms are the fruiting bodies of fungi that are feeding on decaying organic matter. Potassium bicarbonate at the same rate will also work and is better for the soil.

ST. AUGUSTINE

Q. My St. Augustinegrass has long runners that grow along the top of the grass. Mowing doesn't get rid of them. I knew that I had an excessive buildup of thatch, and I had my yard aerated, thinking this might help, but it hasn't so far. How can I get rid of these unattractive things, other than just cutting them off by hand?

A. Surface runners on St. Augustine are common, especially when the fertility is high. Cut back on the number of applications and use the naturally slow-release organic fertilizers. Also add Texas greensand at 40 pounds per 1,000 square feet and lava sand at 80 pounds per 1,000 square feet.

WEEDING

Q. I have lots of weeds in my yard and find hand weeding an overwhelming task. I was thinking of lining some of the beds with a weed-blocking fabric and then putting mulch on top. You have recommended against using the fabric. Why is this?

A. Plastic fabrics block the natural interface between the mulch and the soil. This surface is the important part of the soil. It's there that fascinating biological activity occurs if mulch or cover crops are in place. The surface of the soil beneath mulch is where the moisture is ideal, the pH is ideal, the chemistry is balanced, the light is perfect, the temperature is just right, and the beneficial microbes and other life forms are flourishing. This is where the earthworms and insects travel back and forth between the soil and the mulch, pulling the decaying organic matter down into the soil. This marvelous natural system is physically blocked by weed-blocking-type fabrics or any other artificial material. Plus—when plastic breaks down in the soil, what is released? I don't know for sure, either.

ZOYSIA

Q. Would you recommend the zoysia 'Crowne' or 'Palisades' varieties? I have read about this seed in the *Dallas Planting Manual,* and in one of your books you mention zoysia 'Meyer' as well. I have a densely shaded acre with about two hundred trees. I do have some St. Augustine that survived no previous watering because it was over the septic tank lateral lines and a little bit of Bermuda in my limited sunny spots. Fescue seems to require more water than the zoysia—what do you think?

A. Zoysia is a good grass for low-use areas in full sun. Do not buy mail order—deal with the local suppliers. It must be planted from solid sod and will not grow well in shade. It is not highly drought tolerant. Fescue probably does require even more water.

Q. I am seriously considering ordering grass plugs for zoysia grass from a magazine ad.

A. Bad idea. You should buy grass from local suppliers—plus, zoysia is a very slow-growing grass and must be planted as solid sod. It also can't take much abuse. Wear and tear from kids, pets, or even normal foot traffic kills it quickly. It also won't grow in the shade. Zoysiagrass planted by solid sod, and in a spot that's to be admired and not used, will do well.

Indoor Houseplants

Indoor plants are not only good-looking, they also provide a valuable service. They help clean the air and improve the health of interior environments. Well-selected interior plants are easy to grow with the organic program if you avoid two common mistakes—overfertilizing and overwatering.

The easiest of the interior plants to grow include:

Aloe	*Aloe vera* or *Aloe barbadensis*
Bamboo palm	*Chamaedorea seifrizii*
Chinese evergreen	*Aglaonema* spp.
Corn plant	*Dracaena fragrans* 'Massangeana'
Dumb cane	*Dieffenbachia* spp.
Janet Craig dracaena	*Dracaena deremensis* 'Janet Craig'
Lady palm	*Rhapis excelsa*
Peace lily	*Spathiphyllum* spp.
Pothos	*Epipremnum aureum*
Rubber plant	*Ficus robusta*
Snakeplant	*Sansevieria trifasciata*
War dracaena	*Dracaena* 'Warneckii'

The biggest mistakes I see on maintenance of interior plants are too much water and too much fertilizer. Watering once a week is usually too often and so is fertilizing monthly. Use gentle organic fertilizers and not often. Earthworm castings and lava sand work well in the beginning, and a mild drench of Garrett Juice from time to time is usually enough. If you want a definite schedule, here's one, but it's not that critical.

Immediately after purchase of your interior plants, do the following:

Remove all the Osmocote fertilizer. That's the stuff that looks
like fish eggs.
Add ⅛ inch lava sand and ¼ inch earthworm castings and a
very thin layer of cornmeal.
Monthly—water only as needed and add 1 tablespoon of
apple cider vinegar per gallon.
Quarterly—add Garrett Juice to the irrigation water at
2 ounces per gallon.

POTTING SOIL

The following mix is my latest formula for potted plants. It
is very powerful and needs little if any additional fertilizer.

10 parts compost (Bovinite)
6 parts decomposed granite
4 parts lava sand
4 parts cedar flakes
1 part Texas greensand
½ part dry molasses
½ part cornmeal

BONSAI

**Q. I'm a bonsai grower and do mostly Japanese black pine.
This summer, I had a rash of tree deaths whose symptoms and
pathology were identical to that of pine wilt. My questions is,
which beetles (or other insects) in our area carry these nematodes? Has pine wilt been a problem for Asian pines in our area?**

A. Neither fungal diseases nor nematodes are the primary
problem. Plant stress leads to both situations. Japanese black pine
is not as well adapted here in North Texas as we originally thought.
Austrian seems to be considerably better, but both would be in
stress in the bonsai plantings. Synthetic fertilizer or too much of
any kind of fertilizer can be the root cause. If you aren't already do-

ing so, restrict your fertilizer to the very mild choices, such as earthworm castings, composted manures, compost teas, and any of the blends that contain horticultural cornmeal. Mild drenches of orange oil (d-limonene) will take out the harmful nematodes if present. Filtering the bonsai irrigation water will also help. If that can't be done, add 1 tablespoon of apple cider vinegar per gallon of irrigation water. If the disease problems are bacterial, use peroxide sprays or drenches or the commercial products sold as Consan 20 or Triple Action 20. These are alcohol-based products.

FICUS TREES

Q. We have an indoor potted ficus tree that has a skinny, weak trunk and is falling over without a stake. How can we strengthen and grow this trunk?

A. Add lava sand, Texas greensand, and earthworm castings to the soil, and 1 tablespoon of apple cider vinegar per gallon to the irrigation water. Another product that will help trunk strength is sulpo-mag. Use about 1 tablespoon per gallon of potting soil. Make sure the plant is getting plenty of light and not being overwatered.

Q. My ficus plant has some sort of sticky substance on the leaves but otherwise looks in good condition. I tried washing the leaves, but it's hard to get them all and the results don't last long. I also tried an insecticide recommended for inside plants. It didn't seem to help at all. The problem is bad enough that the floor around the plant gets sticky.

A. Sometimes insect infestations like yours have resulted from unhealthy roots, related stress, and resulting root fungi. Gently work a ⅛–¼-inch layer of horticultural cornmeal into the surface of the soil and spray the foliage with one of the citrus pest control products like Orange Guard. Make sure the plant gets plenty of light and don't overwater or overfertilize. The cornmeal in this case will replace the need for any further fertilization for at least six months. After that, use a monthly drench of Garrett Juice at half strength.

Wildlife/Animals

Animals are as important as the plants in the balance of nature. Natural biodiversity always contains both plants and animals. There are, however, animals that we like and want to encourage and those that are pests and need to be controlled.

ARMADILLOS

Tip from a Reader

I think I found a way to discourage armadillos. I built a golf green in my pasture, and (during the drought) an armadillo took up residence near the green and of course plowed it every night for about two months. I bought a large 16-ounce container of ground red pepper and sprinkled the green. The armadillo came back that night and rooted only two holes. It then continued to root in the yard and pasture but has never returned to the golf green. It might be worth a try for others who don't want these beasts destroyed.

BIRDS

Q. Should we continue to put out bird feed during the winter? I had always heard not to put out feed so the birds would migrate, but I know there are birds that are around all winter, and I don't want them to go hungry.

A. Birds are smarter than that. They'll go when and if it is time. The food we put out is just a supplement, and I recommend you continue to feed the birds.

Q. We have blackbirds pecking away at our pecans. There is a spray that can be used. If we don't get rid of them, there won't be any pecans left to harvest.

A. Birds don't like soap, and Dr. Bronner's Peppermint Soap is the best I've found for repelling various animals. If you actually hit some of the birds with the spray, they'll usually spread the word and not be back. We certainly don't want to hurt the birds, but we can't let them have all the pecans. It's not fair. This technique also works to solve a roosting problem. Use about 1 tablespoon of liquid soap per gallon of spray.

Q. I have a woodpecker that is trying to beat my house down. He even gets in my attic. Any suggestions on how to keep him away from the house without harming him?

A. Spraying the house with garlic-pepper tea or one of the other hot pepper mixes will probably get the beautiful bird to look for other peckables.

Sunflower Seed Hulls

Q. Is there anything toxic in sunflower seed hulls? I love to feed the squirrels and birds, and we have lost a lot of grass in the feeding area. I try to keep the hulls swept and raked. There is also a big pecan tree in the same area. Could either be the problem?

A. The pecan leaves are not the problem; on the contrary, they are beneficial to the soil. The sunflower seeds, however, can be a problem. The seed hulls do have growth-retarding properties and can cause the bare spots you're seeing. Move the feeders around or put them over paved surfaces, a cluster of stepping stones, or gravel. Decomposed granite is my favorite material for this use.

BUTTERFLY GARDENS

Q. Is a butterfly garden just a garden of planted wildflowers or what? When is a good time to start one?

A. The secret to a successful butterfly garden is to plant lots of different flowering plants and be totally organic, but be sure to include lantana, butterfly bush (*Buddleia*), butterfly weed (*Asclepias*), pentas, passion vine, dill, fennel, and parsley. A tree that will attract the beautiful swallowtails is the tickle tongue or prickly ash (*Zanthoxylum*).

DOGS AND CATS

One of the events I'm the most proud of is helping bring the Muenster pet foods to the market. The number of reports I get from people about their animals' health improving is very satisfying. Ronnie Felderhoff, his family, and the staff at Muenster Milling in Muenster, Texas, took a big risk in agreeing to try the Dirt Doctor's recommendations. Muenster Natural dog food and cat food are the only pet foods that have natural diatomaceous earth in the product at the right level and contain no toxic chemical preservatives. For information, call 1-800-772-7178 or check the web site at www.muenstermilling.com.

LIZARDS

Q. I would like to know what I can spray or put out for lizards. They are out in my shop and sometimes come in the house when you open the door, but I have not found the nest.

A. Congratulations, they are one of the most beneficial animals you can have on your property. They eat roaches, crickets, grasshoppers, katydids, and other pests.

MICE AND RATS

Mice are easy to run off. Get rid of or protect the water and food that is attracting them and dust hot pepper such as cayenne. They do not like it at all. Rats can be controlled with Quintox or Rampage if you have severe problems.

SNAKES

Q. We recently found a snake in our back yard near our compost pile. We were told by a friend that compost piles attract snakes. Is this true, and is there anything we can do to prevent

them in our yard? We live in a new subdivision with houses around us.

A. Properly maintained compost piles don't attract snakes any more than other parts of a healthy garden. Most are beneficial non-poisonous snakes. They are all hunters and a great help in controlling rodents. The only poisonous snakes in this part of the country are copperheads, rattlesnakes, water moccasins, and coral snakes. They are distinctive and easy to identify. They are also more afraid of you than you are of them and aren't aggressive unless threatened (accidentally or on purpose). Strongly fragrant materials such as hot pepper, mustard powder, tobacco, and fresh cedar flakes may help make the serpents move on. Quineas (guinea fowl) and roadrunners will definitely solve the problem.

TURTLES

Report from a Reader

I have discovered over the last twenty years that our native North Texas box turtles (three-toed and ornate) effectively control slugs in the garden. They hunt them down in the early morning when the plants are covered with dew and the slugs are out. They also keep crickets and grasshoppers in check: I put a small (about 12 inches above ground and 18 inches underground) wire fence around the garden to contain the turtles. The top of the fence is bent in toward the garden so the turtles cannot climb over it. The turtles require places to hide and burrow, a shallow pan for water, and some additional diversity in their diet, which I provide with fruit scraps and earthworms. They do little or no damage to my vegetables and are delightful.

Appendix

BOOKS AND OTHER PUBLICATIONS

Other Books by the Dirt Doctor

Herbs for Texas offers advice, with the assistance of veteran herbalist Odena Brannam, on growing nearly 150 herbs. Austin: University of Texas Press, 2001; 800-252-3206.

Howard Garrett's Plants for Texas covers native and adapted ornamental and food-crop plants. Arranged alphabetically and cross-referenced for ease of finding detailed information. Austin: University of Texas Press, 1996; 800-252-3206.

Howard Garrett's Texas Organic Gardening (revised) provides organic information specifically for Texas, including plant varieties, planting instructions, and maintenance techniques. Houston: Gulf Publishing, 1998. Available from National Book Network, 800-462-6420.

The Organic Manual (revised) is an easy-to-follow, money-saving guide on the proper selection, installation, and maintenance of organic landscaping and gardening. Irving, Tex.: Tapestry Press, 2002; 972-399-8856.

Plants of the Metroplex (newly revised) has over 300 color photos of landscape plants plus information on the selection, cultivation, uses, and problems of each plant. Austin: University of Texas Press, 1998; 800-252-3206.

Texas Bug Book, coauthored with Malcolm Beck, provides detailed information on the most troublesome and the most helpful bugs, including pictures, life cycle, habitat, and controls. Austin: University of Texas Press, 1999; 800-252-3206.

Texas Gardening the Natural Way: The Complete Handbook. A complete, state-of-the-art organic gardening handbook for Texas. Austin: University of Texas Press, 2003; 800-252-3206.

Texas Organic Vegetable Gardening, coauthored with Malcolm Beck, covers food crops, including vegetables, fruits, nuts, and herbs. Lanham, Md.: Lone Star Books. Available from National Book Network, 800-462-6420.

Acres U.S.A. Publications

Acres U.S.A., a monthly publication, is one of the best on eco-agriculture; 1-800-355-5313. Ask for their 80-page catalog. Some of my favorite Acres books are:

The Albrecht Papers by William Albrecht (1975); four volumes, but especially Vol. 2.

Bread from Stones by Julius Hensel (1991)

Growing Great Garlic by Ron L. Engeland (1991)

Nature's Silent Music by Philip S. Callahan (1992)

Science in Agriculture by Arden Anderson (2000)

The Secret Life of Compost by Malcolm Beck (1997)

Weeds: Control without Poisons by Charles Walters (1999)

Other Valuable Publications

Alexander, Martin. *Introduction to Soil Microbiology.* 2d ed. New York: John Wiley & Sons, 1977.

Beck, Malcolm. *The Garden-Ville Method: Lessons in Nature.* By the king of compost, Malcolm Beck, one of the most knowledgeable people on organics in the country. San Antonio: Garden-Ville, 1998; 800-858-5699.

Carson, Rachel. *Silent Spring.* This is a must-read. If you don't convert to organics after reading this classic, you never will. Cambridge, Mass.: The Riverside Press, 1962.

Diggs, George, Jr., Barney Lipscomb, and Robert J. O'Kennon. *Shiner & Mahler's Illustrated Flora of North Central Texas.* Fort Worth: Botanical Research Institute of Texas and Austin College, 1999.

Fallon, Sally, with Mary G. Enig. *Nourishing Traditions.* 2d ed. Unites the wisdom of ancients with the latest independent scientific research. Provides over 700 delicious recipes that will please gourmets and busy parents. Winona Lake, Ind.: New Trends Publishing, 1999; http://www.newtrendspublishing.com/

Fukuoka, Masanobu. *The One-Straw Revolution.* An introduction to natural farming and an excellent book on the philosophy and practicality of organic gardening from one of Japan's living legends. Emmaus, Pa.: Rodale Press, 1978.

Howard, Sir Albert. *Agricultural Testament* (Emmaus, Pa.: Rodale Press, reissued 1973) and *The Soil and Health* (New York: Devin-Adair, 1947; Schocken Books, 1972). State-of-the-art guides to organic agriculture and the use of compost to bring soil back to health. They were written in the 1940s but are still two of the best publications on the market.

Jackson, William R. *Humic, Fulvic, and Microbial Balance: Organic Soil Conditioning.* Evergreen, Col.: Jackson Research Center, 1993; 800-236-5172.

Olkowski, William, Sheila Daar, and Helga Olkowski. *Common-Sense Pest Control.* An excellent reference for low-toxicity pest control. Newtown, Conn.: Taunton Press, 1991.

Rateaver, Bargyla. *The Organic Method Primer UPDATE* (1994), one of the most comprehensive books, and *Organic Method Primer* (1994), both self-published by Bargyla Rateaver, 9049 Covina Street, San Diego, CA 92126.

Robinson, Jo. *Why Grass-Fed Is Best!* A wonderful little book about the health benefits of eating grass-fed animals and eggs. It is easy to read and well documented. Vashon, Wash.: Vashon Island Press, 2000; 206-436-4156.

Savory, Allan. *Holistic Resource Management.* For anyone involved in the management of land. This book teaches you how to think and treat people and their environment as a whole. Washington, D.C.: Island Press, 1988.

Senn, T. L. *Seaweed and Plant Growth.* Explains in detail the wonderful powers of seaweed as a fertilizer, growth stimulator, and pest repellent. Hastings, New Zealand: Touchwood Books, 1987; www.touchwoodbooks.co.nz.

The Stockman Grass Farmer, a monthly publication from the Mississippi Valley Publishing Corp., 282 Commerce Park Drive, Ridgeland, MS 39157, 800-748-9808; http://www.stockmangrassfarmer.com/

Stout, Ruth. *How to Have a Green Thumb without an Aching Back* (New York: Exposition Press, 1955), *Gardening without Work* (New York: Devin-Adair, 1961), and *The Ruth Stout No-Work Gardening Book* (Emmaus, Pa.: Rodale Press, 1971) are great. Stout was a humorous writer, a philosopher, and an advocate of mulching.

Whitcomb, Carl. *Establishment and Maintenance of Landscape Plants.* Provides excellent research and backup for the practical approach to horticulture. Stillwater, Okla.: Lacebark Publications, 1991.

Wilson, Duff. *Fateful Harvest: The True Story of a Small Town, a Global Industry and a Toxic Secret.* New York: Harper Collins Publishers, 2001; www.harpercollins.com

FORMULAS

Baking Soda Fungicide

Mix 4 teaspoons—about 1 rounded tablespoon—of baking soda and 1 tablespoon of horticultural oil into one gallon of water. Spray lightly on foliage of plants afflicted with black spot, powdery mildew, brown patch, and other fungal diseases. Avoid overusing or pouring on the soil. Potassium bicarbonate is a good substitute for baking soda. Citrus oil or molasses can be used instead of horticultural oil.

Garlic Teas

To make garlic-pepper tea, liquefy 2 whole bulbs of garlic and 2 hot peppers in a blender ½ to ⅔ full of water. Strain the solids and add enough water to the garlic-pepper juice to make 1 gallon of concentrate. Use ¼ cup of concentrate per gallon of spray. To make garlic tea, simply omit the pepper and add another bulb of garlic. Add 2 tablespoons of blackstrap molasses for more control.

Garrett Juice

1 cup of compost tea or liquid humate
1 ounce each of vinegar, molasses, and seaweed

To make your own homemade concentrate, mix:

1 gallon of compost tea or liquid humate
1 pint natural apple cider vinegar
1 pint blackstrap molasses
1 pint liquid seaweed

Use 1½ cups of this concentrate per gallon of spray.

Garrett Juice—Ready to Spray

My recommended basic organic foliar spray is available commercially, or you can make your own. Mix the following ingredients in a gallon of water:

1 cup manure-based compost tea
1 ounce liquid molasses
1 ounce natural apple cider vinegar
1 ounce liquid seaweed

For disease and insect control, add:

¼ cup garlic tea or
¼ cup garlic-pepper tea, or
1 ounce of orange oil

For homemade fire ant killer, add:

2 ounces of citrus oil per gallon of Garrett Juice

The ready-to-use solution should not have more than 2 ounces of orange oil per gallon.

Manure Compost Tea

Fill any container half full of manure-based compost, and then fill to the top with water. Let the mix sit for ten to fourteen days. Pumping air into the concentrate with a simple aquarium pump makes an even better product. Dilute and strain. A rule of thumb is to dilute the leachate down to one part compost liquid to four to ten parts water. It should look like iced tea. Strain the solids out using old pantyhose, cheesecloth, or row-cover material. Spray on the foliage of all plants, including fruit trees, perennials, annuals, vegetables, and roses—especially those that are regularly attacked by insects or fungal pests. It's very effective on black spot on roses and early blight on toma-toes. Add 2 tablespoons of molasses to each gallon of spray for more power. Add citrus oil for even greater pest-killing power.

Milk Fungicide

Mix ½ cup of skim milk in a gallon of water and spray.

Organic Herbicides

Here are two versions:

1 gallon full-strength 10 percent vinegar
½ cup orange oil
1 teaspoon Dr. Bronner's or other mild liquid soap
Yucca extract at a higher rate is even better

Or

1 gallon full-strength 10 percent vinegar
½ cup orange oil
1 cup liquid molasses
1 teaspoon Basic H or other mild soap or yucca extract

Potting Soil

I keep fine-tuning my potting soil mixture. Here are my lat-est versions.

#1

10 parts compost
6 parts peat moss or Bovinite
4 parts lava sand
4 parts granite sand

4 parts cedar flakes
2 parts earthworm castings
1 part Texas greensand
1 part horticultural cornmeal
½ part sul-po-mag
½ part dry molasses

#2

8 parts compost
4 parts peat moss or Bovinite
4 parts lava sand
2 parts decomposed granite sand
2 parts cedar flakes
1 part zeolite
1 part horticultural cornmeal
1 part dry molasses
1 part Texas greensand

Skunk Solution

If your pet tangles with the wrong end of a skunk, here's a nontoxic, effective, and inexpensive way to get rid of the odor, and you can keep these ingredients on hand all the time. Mix:

1 quart of hydrogen peroxide
¼ cup baking soda
1 teaspoon of liquid soap

Rub the mixture into the fur, taking care to avoid the pet's ears and eyes. Leave it on until the odor diminishes. Then rinse it off thoroughly.

Caution: Do not store this mixture.

Tree Trunk Goop

Mix one part each of natural diatomaceous earth, soft rock phosphate, and manure-based compost in enough water to make it sloppy. (Premixed Tree Trunk Goop is available at many organic suppliers.) Fireplace ashes can be used in lieu of soft rock phosphate. Put it onto cuts, borer holes, or other injuries on trunks or limbs. Reapply if washed off by rain or irrigation. Don't worry. It's good for the soil.

Vinegar Fungicide

Mix 3 tablespoons of natural apple cider vinegar in 1 gallon of water. Spray during the cool part of the day for black spot on roses and other fungal diseases. Adding molasses at 1 tablespoon per gallon will help.

Wheat Bran/Cornmeal/Molasses Blend

60 percent wheat bran
30 percent cornmeal
10 percent dry molasses

Sick Tree Treatment

1. *Remove excess soil from above root ball.* A very high percentage of trees have been planted too low. Soil on top of the root ball smothers the tree and leads to circling and girdling roots. Soil, or even heavy mulch, on trunks keeps the bark constantly moist, which can rot or girdle the tree.
2. *Aerate the root zone heavily.* Start between the dripline and the trunk and go far out beyond the dripline. A 7–12-inch depth of the aeration holes is ideal, but any depth is beneficial. An alternative is to spray the root zone with a living organism product or biostimulant.
3. *Apply Texas greensand* at about 40–80 pounds/1,000 square feet, lava sand at about 40–80 pounds/1,000 square feet, horticultural cornmeal at about 10–20 pounds/1,000 square feet, and sugar or dry molasses at about 5 pounds/1,000 square feet. Cornmeal is a natural disease fighter, and sugar is a carbon source to feed the microbes in the soil.
4. *Apply a 1-inch layer of compost,* followed by a 3–5-inch layer of shredded native tree trimmings. Native cedar is

the best source for mulch. In turf, use a 1-inch layer of horticultural cedar flakes.

5. *Spray foliage and soil monthly or more often if possible with Garrett Juice* (see formula above). For large-scale farms and ranches, a one-time spraying is beneficial if the budget doesn't allow for ongoing sprays. Adding garlic tea to the spray is also beneficial while the tree is in trouble.

6. *Stop using high-nitrogen fertilizers and toxic chemical pesticides.* Pesticides kill the beneficial nematodes and insects. Fake fertilizers are destructive to the chemistry, the structure, and the life in the soil.

I hope you enjoy the Natural Way!

Index